The Bonds
of Freedom

The Bonds of Freedom

Simone de Beauvoir's Existentialist Ethics

KRISTANA ARP

OPEN COURT
Chicago and La Salle, Illinois

To order books from Open Court, call 1-800-815-2280.

Open Court Publishing Company is a division of Carus Publishing Company.

© 2001 by Carus Publishing Company

First printing 2001

Printed and bound in the United States of America.

Library of Congress Cataloging-in-Publication Data

Arp, Kristana.
    The bonds of freedom : Simone de Bouvoir's existentialist ethics / Kristana
    Arp.
        p. cm.
    Includes bibliographical references (p.) and index.
    ISBN 0-8126-9442-2 – ISBN 0-8126-9443-0 (pbk.)
      1. Beauvoir, Simone de, 1908– Pour une morale de l'ambiguité.
    2. Existential ethics.   I. Title
    B2430.B343 P6833 2001
    171'.2—dc21   2001036227

To my father, Halton Arp,
who taught me to persevere

Table of Contents

Acknowledgments

Any academic woman of my generation owes a great deal to the women who went before her. I want to mention one woman in particular who helped pave the way for a book like this: Margaret A. Simons. Once upon a time philosophers did not write on Beauvoir; they wrote on Jean-Paul Sartre. Peg has devoted her career to writing on Beauvoir and encouraged many others to do so. Sonia Kruks and Robert Stone also did important work on Beauvoir early on. All three of these people have had some input into the present work. Peg Simons has given moral support and advice throughout the many years it took to complete it. Bob Stone read a draft of chapter 6 and made useful comments. Sonia Kruks delivered a commentary on a paper I gave on Beauvoir's *The Ethics of Ambiguity* in spring 1997. (My friend Julie Ward organized this session.) I first read *The Second Sex* as a philosophical text in a class of hers I sat in at The New School for Social Research in the early 1980s. I want to thank them all.

Over the last ten years other people have also published ground-breaking work on Beauvoir's philosophy. Among these authors are: Debra Bergoffen, Eva Lundgren-Gothlin, Karen Vintges, Kate and Edward Fullbrook, and Sara Heinämaa. I have read them all with keen interest, although I do not always agree with their interpretations. I have enjoyed getting to know them at sessions and conferences devoted to Beauvoir's work. Many of these sessions were organized by the Simone de Beauvoir Circle, an informal group of philosophers working on Beauvoir that lately has been run by Barbara Andrews. Lester Embree's symposium on The Phenomenology of Simone de Beauvoir in 1997 also provided an important forum. Another group, the New

York Chapter of The Society for Women in Philosophy (SWIP), has been an important source of support for me. I presented a rough draft of material in chapter 5 to their Ethics Discussion Group in 1995. I have also learned a great deal from the books that have been written on Sartrean ethics. Interchanges with three of these authors—Thomas Anderson, Linda Bell, and William McBride—led me to hone my ideas further.

Esther Hyneman and Ken Bernard, colleagues at Long Island University, Brooklyn, read drafts of chapters. Another colleague, John Ehrenberg, informed me about publishers. My colleagues in the philosophy department also contributed. My prose is better for Margaret Cuonzo's advice. Joseph Filonowicz arranged for me to deliver part of chapter 4 at a meeting of The Long Island Philosophical Society, which he heads. (Gertrude Postl was my commentator.) Howard Ponzer prepared an early version of the bibliography. Two anonymous referees for Open Court made comments on the manuscript that were extremely helpful. It has been a delight to work with my editor at Open Court, Kerri Mommer. I thank them all.

My love and gratitude go to my stepmother, Susanna Dakin, who carefully read and commented on the entire first draft of the manuscript. And special thanks go to other special people in my life.

Finally, I must thank the former Research Release Time Committee of Long Island University, Brooklyn, which reduced my teaching load during part of the time I was working on this book. I also appreciate the support of the Provost of the Brooklyn Campus, Gale Stevens Haynes.

*   *   *   *   *

Parts of my article "Simone de Beauvoir's Existentialist Ontology," *Philosophy Today* 43, no. 3 (Fall 1999): 266-71 are reprinted here with the kind permission of the publisher.

List of Abbreviations

I have used these abbreviations to refer to the following works in the body of the text.

AMM   Simone de Beauvoir, *All Men Are Mortal*, trans. Leonard N. Friedman (New York: W. W. Norton & Company, 1992).

BN   Jean-Paul Sartre, *Being and Nothingness*, trans. Hazel Barnes (New York: Philosophical Library, 1956).

BO   Simone de Beauvoir, *The Blood of Others*, trans. Roger Senhouse and Yvonne Moyse (New York: Pantheon Books, 1983).

DS I   Simone de Beauvoir, *Le Deuxième Sexe*, Vol. I (Paris: Gallimard, 1949). My translations.

DS II   Simone de Beauvoir, *Le Deuxième Sexe*, Vol. II (Paris: Gallimard, 1949). My translations.

EA   Simone de Beauvoir, *The Ethics of Ambiguity*, trans. Bernard Frechtman (New York: Carol Publishing Group, 1991).

ESN   Simone de Beauvoir, "L'Existentialisme et la sagesse des nations" in *L'Existentialisme et la sagesse des nations* (Paris: Les Éditions Nagel, 1986). My translations.

IMRP   Simone de Beauvoir, "Idéalisme moral et réalisme politique" in *L'Existentialisme et la sagesse des nations* (Paris: Les Éditions Nagel, 1986). My translations.

OPO   Simone de Beauvoir, "Oeil pour oeil" in *L'Existentialisme et la sagesse des nations* (Paris: Les Éditions Nagel, 1986). My translations.

PC   Simone de Beauvoir, *Pyrrhus et Cinéas* (Paris: Gallimard, 1944). My translations.

TSS   Simone de Beauvoir, *The Second Sex*, trans. H. M. Parshley (New York: Vintage Books, 1989).

WSD   Simone de Beauvoir, *Who Shall Die*, trans. Claude Francis and Fernande Gontier (Florissant, MO: River Press, 1983).

Why Beauvoir's Ethics?

Simone de Beauvoir was one of the most famous female intellectuals of the twentieth century. Although she was one of the first women to receive a higher degree in philosophy in France and taught philosophy for a number of years, she is not generally known as a philosopher. She herself swore in her memoirs and interviews that she was not one. She had a very limiting definition of what a philosopher was. A philosopher for her was someone who constructed a philosophical system, as her companion Jean-Paul Sartre did in his magnum opus *Being and Nothingness*. He was the philosopher, not she. She even claimed that all of her philosophical ideas came from him. Like some other writers who have written on Beauvoir recently, I see no reason to accept this characterization. Beauvoir was not a system builder, but she wrote some explicitly philosophical works in the 1940s. These works, especially the work this book centers on, present philosophical ideas of importance and originality. In this book I explicate these ideas, view them in the context of wider debates and defend them from some possible objections.

Other writers who have taken Beauvoir seriously as a philosopher claim to find a distinctive philosophy expressed in the entire corpus of her work taken as a whole. The scope of this book is somewhat more limited, but its thesis is not for that reason less significant. My claim is that one of Beauvoir's most important contributions to philosophy is to have constructed an existentialist ethics, that is, an ethics based on the central tenets of existentialism. Existentialism sees humans as beings who create and define themselves in interaction with others and the circumstances they find themselves in. Beauvoir's accomplishment is significant, for one thing, because critics of existentialism charge that an ethics could not be founded on such a philosophy. They see existentialism's insistence that all values are human creations as reason for rejecting it. Beauvoir's ethics is also the most philosophically consistent and workable version of an existentialist ethics. In chapter 5 I consider whether it is correct to say that Sartre developed an ethics, at least an ethics based on the philosophy of *Being and Nothingness*. I conclude that it is not. A number of books have been written on Sartre's ethics, however, which, whether Sartre did or not, do present a version of existentialist ethics. I discuss the problems these versions of existentialist ethics run into and show how Beauvoir's ethics avoids them.

Because this is a book on Beauvoir's existentialist ethics, it focuses primarily on one text, *The Ethics of Ambiguity*. This work, published in 1947, comes at the end of what Beauvoir calls her moral period, the time that she was searching for a foundation for her judgments about the events leading up to and culminating in World War II. I describe these events and their effect on her in chapter 2. During this period she wrote a series of essays, novels, and one play addressing moral issues. In chapter 3 I discuss how these texts connect to *The Ethics of Ambiguity*. I contend that *The Ethics of Ambiguity* is the decisive text as far as her ethics is concerned. First, it represents the culmination of her thought on this subject. Secondly, only in this work does she provide the theoretical foundation required for an ethics.

In *The Ethics of Ambiguity* Beauvoir sketches out her own distinctive theory of freedom. She introduces a new conception of freedom, moral freedom, into existentialism. Moral freedom is different from ontological freedom, the type of freedom that Sartre emphasizes in *Being and Nothingness* all humans always possess. It is also different from what Beauvoir calls power, by which she means the freedom from material and social constraints. Unlike ontological freedom, our power can be limited by outside forces. Moral freedom is different from these other two types of freedom, but is also connected to them. Moral freedom is the conscious affirmation of one's ontological freedom. And it can only be developed in the absence of certain constraints. Most importantly, however, developing moral freedom requires assuming a certain sort of relation to other people. As

Beauvoir says, in order to be genuinely free, one needs others to be free as well. My attaining moral freedom depends on others being able to attain it.

Here I want to highlight only briefly how by introducing a specifically moral level of freedom into existentialism Beauvoir solves the central problem that an existentialist ontology poses for ethics. As I said, existentialism's rejection of objective values alarmed its critics. If all values are creations of human freedom, how can any one value have priority over any other? And if this is the case, how is moral judgment possible?[1] Advocates of existentialist ethics reply that, since all values are grounded in human freedom, ethics itself should be grounded in freedom. But this solution, critics continue, seems to be ruled out in turn by the existentialist conception of freedom—at least by Sartre's conception of it. In *Being and Nothingness* Sartre dramatically proclaims that human freedom is absolute: it is present in every situation and cannot be diminished. So all humans are equally free, because absolutely free. But all humans do not act morally, certainly.

Beauvoir comes to existentialism's rescue and solves this problem by positing another level of freedom, moral freedom, a level that not all people achieve. Indeed they must constantly struggle to attain it by subjecting their actions to moral scrutiny. Furthermore, Beauvoir shows how an individual can only develop moral freedom by interacting with other morally free subjects. I lay out an argument for this thesis in chapter 4. Since my moral freedom is dependent on that of others, an obligation to help or at least not hinder others' attainment of it is built into my own quest for it. The questions of how one should treat others and why one should treat them this way are central to moral theory, of course. Beauvoir answers that one should promote the moral freedom of others in order to enjoy it oneself.

The difference in scope is not the only difference between this book and other recent books on Beauvoir's philosophy. My interpretation of Beauvoir's thought differs as well. Some of these writers present an interpretation of her thought that, while original and interesting, leads them to distort the position that Beauvoir takes in *The Ethics of Ambiguity*.

For instance, Karen Vintges in her book translated from the Dutch as *Philosophy as Passion* surveys Beauvoir's entire œuvre, not just her philosophical essays, to show how her philosophical concerns turned from ontology to ethics over time. But the ethics that Beauvoir ended up espousing was not the ethics of *The Ethics of Ambiguity*, according to Vintges. It was not an existentialist ethics at all, but rather an "art of living" ethics, an approach to ethics that Vintges connects with ideas subsequently expressed by Michel Foucault. Vintges finds this idea of ethics as an art of living first expressed in Beauvoir's novel *The Mandarins* published in 1956. This type of ethics is a very personal ethics. Each person creates him or herself individually. This is what Beauvoir did in her memoirs, which Vintges sees as her mode of "ethical self-creation," as well as in her letters and diaries.[2]

Vintges rightly intuits that this approach to ethics is at odds with the position that Beauvoir takes in *The Ethics of Ambiguity*. She holds that Beauvoir rejected the ethical stance of *The Ethics of Ambiguity* later in life, repeating the criticisms that Beauvoir made of this work in her memoirs. However, these later remarks of Beauvoir must be taken in context, as I point out in chapter 2. In any case, Beauvoir's position in *The Ethics of Ambiguity* must be evaluated on its own merits. Vintges judges the work to be severely flawed. In it she sees Beauvoir to fall back into the same Kantian style of ethics she criticizes by formulating ethical rules, rules that are "prescriptive," "unequivocal," and "absolute."[3] However, Vintges is wrong; Beauvoir does not offer any rules like these there. She does sketch out what she calls a method for sorting out the options facing one when making difficult decisions, but it only recommends certain ways of approaching such dilemmas, and is hardly decisive.[4] Since Vintges endorses an entirely different sort of ethics that she ascribes to Beauvoir, it is not surprising that she rejects the ethics put forward in *The Ethics of Ambiguity*. But she does not do so for good reasons.

Another book that presents an original and interesting interpretation of Beauvoir's thought is *The Philosophy of Simone de Beauvoir* by Debra Bergoffen. Bergoffen claims to hear two different voices speaking in Beauvoir's work as a whole: a dominant one, her "existential" voice, and a muted one stressing joy and spontaneity that espouses an ethics of generosity.[5] Obviously the ethics I analyze and defend in this book is the one Bergoffen associates with Beauvoir's dominant voice. I do not dispute that there are these other suggestive aspects to Beauvoir's thought, however.

Bergoffen finds the ethics of generosity sketched out in Beauvoir's muted voice to be much more appealing than her existentialist ethics. But, as with Vintges, her critique of Beauvoir's existentialist ethics rests on a mischaracterization of it. Aside from the ideas expressed by this muted voice, Bergoffen sees "little that is new," in *The Ethics of Ambiguity*, that is, little that is different from Sartre.[6] Although she says that Beauvoir's account of freedom is central to *The Ethics of Ambiguity*, she does not discuss freedom, equating it simply with intentionality, and thus focusing only on ontological freedom. The one advance that Bergoffen sees Beauvoir as having made over Sartre is identifying two moments of intentionality: one dedicated to the disclosure of being and one expressing the desire for being. Bergoffen illegitimately links the Sartrean conception of the project, which defines an individual's personality, with the desire for being. She calls the ethics that Beauvoir propounds in her dominant voice an "ethics of the project," but since Bergoffen sees the project as an expression of the will to achieve being, she rejects this ethics. The project has "imperialistic" inclinations, because it aims to "capture the other's freedom."[7] It is not necessarily wrong to describe Beauvoir's ethics as an ethics of the project, although this is really a Sartrean term. However, Bergoffen's characterization of this ethics is off-base. As I argue in chapter 6, the quest for moral freedom obliges one to fight against those who attempt to "capture" others' freedom (or since their ontological freedom cannot be taken away, to fight against those who try to limit others to this most basic level of freedom.) The way that Beauvoir ties the quest for moral freedom to a commitment to the political liberation of the oppressed makes her ethics literally an anti-imperialistic ethics.

In chapter 2 I discuss how the ethical stance that Beauvoir takes in *The Ethics of Ambiguity* was a response to the events that she witnessed during the war years. Inclined at first toward pacifism, Beauvoir eventually came to recognize the moral imperative for struggle against murderous regimes like the Nazis, even if that struggle turned violent. Hence Beauvoir's ethics is an ethics that privileges action, indeed preaches activism, and scorns passivity. (This condemnation of passivity also marks *The Second Sex*.) Perhaps one could object, as Bergoffen seems to, that Beauvoir goes too far in this direction. One might also question the relevance of such a stance today when, at least in most Western democracies, no comparable evil confronts us. A personal ethics lived out in the context of private life, like the one that Vintges attributes to Beauvoir, might be more in sync with our present circumstances. *The Ethics of Ambiguity* is definitely not an ethics of private life. But that does not make it an "imperialistic" ethics either. It is an ethics of political engagement that is extremely sensitive to the possible negative consequences of involvement in other people's lives.

On the other hand, I agree with much that Eva Lundgren-Gothlin has to say about *The Ethics of Ambiguity* in her study of Beauvoir's philosophy, *Sex and Existence*. She sees *The Ethics of Ambiguity* as offering Beauvoir's "own original interpretation of existentialist phenomenology" and as the place where Beauvoir formulates her ethics.[8] But Lundgren-Gothlin's main focus is *The Second Sex*, not *The Ethics of Ambiguity*. Analyzing its philosophical foundations, she uncovers the Marxist and Hegelian elements of Beauvoir's thought, speculating that Marx's 1844 manuscripts (first published in French in 1937) led Beauvoir to see productive activity to be the way for humans to realize their true humanity, hence Beauvoir's emphasis on women's economic independence in *The Second Sex*. The same influence might account for why Beauvoir sees engaging in joint activities with others as the hallmark of moral freedom in *The Ethics of Ambiguity*.

Lundgren-Gothlin does not recognize that Beauvoir developed a distinct conception of freedom in this work.[9] She does see two different conceptions of freedom at work in *The Second Sex*: an abstract negative freedom, similar to ontological freedom, that women retain and a positive concrete freedom—an amalgam of moral freedom and power or freedom from constraint—that they are deprived of. In chapter 7 I discuss how Beauvoir's conception of moral freedom is pushed into the background in *The Second Sex*. But Beauvoir's distinction between different types of freedom dates to *Pyrrhus et Cinéas*, written in 1944. The conception of a specifically moral level of freedom remains relevant in *The Second Sex*, because it can explain why the oppression of women is morally wrong. It provides a goal for women, and men, to aim at. As Lundgren-Gothlin points out, the existentialist concept of transcendence cannot fill this role because according to Beauvoir men achieve transcendence in spite of their oppression of women.[10]

I also follow Sonia Kruks in seeing Beauvoir's treatment of freedom as the distinctive feature of her work from the 1940s. In pathbreaking work published some years ago Kruks points out how Beauvoir's position on freedom differs from Sartre's position on freedom in *Being and Nothingness*. Sartre highlights humans' ontological freedom, which he claims is indestructible and without limit. Starting in *Pyrrhus et Cinéas* Beauvoir explores the impact that social conditions, in particular one's relation to other people, have on freedom. Kruks recognizes that Beauvoir makes a distinction between ontological freedom and power, which Kruks calls "effective freedom," as early as *Pyrrhus et Cinéas*.[11] Kruks agrees that there is a moral dimension to freedom for Beauvoir because of the way that one person's freedom is connected to another's.[12] But for Kruks the important way that Beauvoir's thought departs from Sartre's is not her conception of moral freedom. Rather it is that Beauvoir holds that to be deprived of power or effective freedom to a sufficient degree diminishes one's ontological freedom. Under conditions of extreme oppression for Beauvoir, Kruks says, "freedom can be reduced to no more than a suppressed potentiality."[13] Sartre rules this out, in *Being and Nothingness*, at least, when he claims that the slave in chains is as free as his master.[14]

My position on this issue is that people, even the most severely oppressed, always retain their ontological freedom. In the context of existentialist ontology this is what makes them human. And it is because they are human beings that it is wrong to treat them in this way. In chapter 6 I hypothesize that what the oppressed are deprived of, in Beauvoir's scheme, is the ability to develop moral freedom. For this hypothesis to be correct there would have to be an underlying connection between having power, that is, being free from certain constraints, and developing moral freedom, an idea I also explore.

Kruks and Lundgren-Gothlin see Beauvoir's philosophical originality to lie in her contributions to social and political philosophy. I highlight her contribution to ethics instead. By introducing a new conception of freedom into existentialism, Beauvoir puts existentialist ethics on a sound philosophical footing. She constructs an ethics consistent with existentialism, one that sees freedom to be both the defining feature of human existence and its ethical ideal. Beauvoir's breakthrough is to change existentialism's focus on one's own freedom into a focus on the freedom of others.[15] Questions about the source and the extent of our responsibilities to others are central to ethics. Beauvoir takes an original position on this issue that merits close attention.

Furthermore, Beauvoir's ethics is very sensitive to the context of human actions. It does not judge them in terms of any overarching principles (in spite of what Vintges says). It takes into account the actual circumstances that people find themselves in. This is due, as I show in the next chapter, to Beauvoir's grounding in the phenomenological tradition and her allegiance to the concept of the situated subject. Beauvoir's approach to ethics thus fits people's actual moral attitudes and practices. For all these reasons the existentialist ethics that Beauvoir puts forward in *The Ethics of Ambiguity* deserves close and sustained analysis.

Beauvoir as Situated
Subject: The Historical
Background

Simone de Beauvoir is a philosopher in the phenomenological tradition. One important contribution of this tradition is its insight that consciousness should not be considered in abstraction from the world it is conscious of. Furthermore, what one is conscious of is always tied to the situation one finds oneself in. One is always rooted in the here and now, a here and now that follows one wherever one may go. But we are not limited to the present. Consciousness always stretches itself back into the past and forward into the future. There is a historical dimension to one's situation as well. One is always born at a particular time and place, in a certain family and social class and assigned a specific gender. All these factors color someone's consciousness of the world. The phenomenological concept of the subject incorporates all these insights. It is a concept of the subject in situation, or, as I prefer to call it, a concept of the situated subject.

The original insight of Edmund Husserl, the founder of phenomenology, is that consciousness is in its essence consciousness *of* something. This is the basis of his concept of intentionality, which he uses as a framework to analyze all mental acts. To do so, he abstracts from all questions about whether the objects that we are conscious of actually exist or not, a question that preoccupied philosophy up to this point.

Martin Heidegger, a student of Husserl's, takes phenomenology in a different direction in *Being and Time*. Heidegger no longer abstracts from questions about existence as Husserl did. On the contrary, he wants to enquire into the nature of being, just like metaphysicians of old. But he does so in a radically new way, asserting, "*only as phenomenology, is ontology possible.*"[1] Heidegger holds that the relation between the subject and the world it is conscious of is so close as to form a "unitary phenomenon" he calls Being-in-the-world.

Maurice Merleau-Ponty was not a German philosopher, but rather one of Simone de Beauvoir's oldest friends and a fellow student and colleague. He was deeply influenced by Husserl's and Heidegger's thought. He even read Husserl's unpublished manuscripts (in particular the text published after Husserl's death as *Ideen II*). In his *Phenomenology of Perception*, published in 1945, he uses the phenomenological method to analyze the role the body plays in perception. He extends Heidegger's unitary phenomenon Being-in-the-world to include three aspects: consciousness, body, and world.

Jean-Paul Sartre's *Being and Nothingness* also reveals the influence of Husserl and Heidegger. Like Merleau-Ponty, Sartre studied Husserl in Germany and wrote earlier works critiquing his ideas.[2] As I discuss in the chapter 4, Sartre reverts to a non-phenomenological ontology, positing two categories of being: being-in-itself and being-for-itself. But Sartre's theory of self-other relations is phenomenological, as it is based on his description of the experience of 'the look'. Under the influence of Husserl and Heidegger, Sartre crafted his own concept of situation. For him, one's situation is the product of the for-itself, or consciousness's engagement in the world.

Beauvoir's Roots in the Phenomenological Tradition

The concept of the situated subject is thus central to the thought of all these philosophers: Husserl, Heidegger, Sartre, and Merleau-Ponty. Beauvoir's thought is also shaped by the conviction that the individual is always a situated subject. For instance, in *The Second Sex* Beauvoir argues that there is no such thing as a female essence. Instead, in order to understand what it means to be a woman, one has to examine different aspects of women's concrete situations, now and in the past. This is the monumental task that Beauvoir takes on in this work, particularly in the second volume, which has a very phenomenological title: "L'Expérience vécue" (Lived Experience).[3]

Beauvoir's allegiance to the concept of the situated subject led her to see the novel as an important mode of expression for philosophical ideas. In a diary she kept when she was nineteen she already was forming her plan to link philosophy with literature.[4] In her essay "Littérature et métaphysique," published in April 1946, she argues that a purely intellectual description cannot give an adequate expression of reality.[5] True to her convictions, Beauvoir wrote a number of philosophical novels. In these novels Beauvoir takes care to construct a context for her characters' ideas that situates them as subjects.

I have recounted how the concept of the situated subject has its roots in Husserl and Heidegger and how it was further developed by Sartre and Merleau-Ponty. Given this genealogy, some might assume that Beauvoir's exposure to this idea and to the whole phenomenological tradition came via Sartre. Such an assumption is fed by Beauvoir's repeated assertions that Sartre, not she, was the philosopher and that he was the sole philosophical influence on her work. But there is ample evidence that Beauvoir encountered the ideas of Husserl and Heidegger directly, not as filtered down through Sartre. For instance, she discussed Husserl with her friend Fernando Gerassi, who was a former student of Husserl's.[6] In her memoirs she records how she studied German in the early 1930s and in 1934 read Husserl's *The Phenomenology of Internal Time-Consciousness* "without too much difficulty."[7] Furthermore, Beauvoir has said that during this period she "was infused with Heidegger's philosophy."[8] Before the war she translated long passages from *Being and Time* for Sartre.[9]

Merleau-Ponty also exerted a significant influence on Beauvoir. Beauvoir wrote a review of his *Phenomenology of Perception* for the fledgling issue of *Les Temps modernes* in October 1945. In it she endorsed his views about the central role of the body in perception, while acknowledging the way that his approach diverges from Sartre. At the end, interestingly enough, she alludes to the relevance of phenomenology to ethics: "Only with it [phenomenology] as a base can one succeed in constructing an ethics which man can totally and sincerely adhere to."[10]

Not long after writing this review, Beauvoir began in *The Ethics of Ambiguity* to sketch out the only ethics she thought appropriate for humans, given the ambiguous nature of their existence. She begins her exposition with a statement she attributes to Sartre: a human is "a being who *makes himself* a lack of being *in order that there might be being*" (EA 11). This statement, although couched in Sartrean language, is really only a restatement of Husserl's theory of intentionality, as I discuss in the next chapter. Thus Beauvoir's ethics is founded in phenomenology, as she claimed in her review of Merleau-Ponty ethics should be. The following chapters reveal how Beauvoir's ethics draws not only from the phenomenological tradition but from the concept of the situated subject itself.

Beauvoir as Situated Subject

The concept of the situated subject obviously influenced Beauvoir's thought. But it also provides a rationale for enquiring into the details of Beauvoir's situation at the time that she wrote *The Ethics of Ambiguity* and her other works on ethics. For Beauvoir the author was a situated subject too: she wrote her works at a specific time and place. In order to fully understand the works, one must take her situation at the time into account. A lot of attention has been paid to Beauvoir's personal life during this period, in particular her romantic relationship with Jean-Paul Sartre.[11] But it was the world historical situation that influenced her ethics, not her personal romantic history.

Beauvoir wrote *The Ethics of Ambiguity* in Paris during the first half of 1946, one and a half years after its liberation from the Nazis. The events leading up to and culminating in World War II had a profound effect on her. In her memoirs she records how they shattered her previous individualistic, self-absorbed world view. She says spring 1939 marked a watershed in her life. But her memoirs show how Beauvoir was also affected by historical events before this turning point.

Beauvoir, who was born and lived in Paris all of her life, was pushed into a teaching career because her aristocratic father's financial failures rendered him unable to provide her with a dowry. This allowed her to live a relatively Bohemian life style for a middle-class woman of her time. When she was studying for her *agregation* in philosophy at the Sorbonne in 1929, she met Jean-Paul Sartre, along with others who would go on to become the leading French intellectuals of their day. She and Sartre went on to become lifelong companions. In France in particular, students and intellectuals commonly identify themselves with the Left. During the 1930s Beauvoir read

Marx, Trotsky, and Rosa Luxemburg; not surprisingly, she and Sartre were Communist sympathizers (although life in the U.S.S.R. seemed dismal to them).[12] In her memoirs she pokes fun at the naiveté of her political views then when, "happily the liquidation of capitalism seemed close at hand," and mocks the excuses she came up with to avoid political commitment.[13]

But there was another important current in French intellectual life during the 1930s. Eva Lundgren-Gothlin, who has done extensive research on this period, points out that Beauvoir was strongly influenced by the anti-militaristic pacifism of a writer known as Alain, as were many other French people.[14] Beauvoir alludes to him several times in the memoirs, but there ascribes her fervent hope that war be avoided to an "obsessional pre-occupation with my own private affairs."[15] Furthermore, Beauvoir was not the only one who refused to face up to the threat posed by the spread of Fascism throughout Europe. The Communists did too; even the Radical Socialists preached pacifism at this time.[16] Beauvoir visited Sartre twice when he was studying in Berlin in 1935. He also denied the portent of what he was witnessing.[17] In retrospect, the events leading up to the Second World War seemed to have followed an inevitable trajectory, but their underlying logic was not visible to those caught up in them at the time.

Whatever pacifist convictions Beauvoir might have had were sorely tested by the Spanish Civil War. She felt personally involved in this "astonishing and epic struggle" because her close friend Fernando Gerassi went off to fight.[18] The left-wing press covered it closely, though not everyone on the Left supported French intervention. Beauvoir certainly did, and was exasperated by the Socialist Popular Front government's refusal to supply arms to the Spanish Republic, or even to open the border so that others could.

However, as Hitler prepared to invade Czechoslovakia Beauvoir still clung to her conviction that war with Germany should be avoided at any cost, although Sartre and Merleau-Ponty argued against her. She was greatly relieved when the Munich Pact was signed, insuring "peace in our time." The Fascists continued to advance across Europe and the Spanish Republicans suffered defeat after defeat. The newspapers revealed the existence of concentration camps, and Beauvoir learned of the persecution of Jews in Germany. The pressure on her grew until finally in spring 1939, she gave up her isolationist stance and affirmed the necessity of war. At this point, she says: "I renounced my individualist, anti-humanist way of life. I learned the value of solidarity."[19] The arguments that she gave seven years later in *The Ethics of Ambiguity* that one's own freedom is connected to that of others undoubtedly were inspired by her revelation at this time that she was "linked by every nerve in me to each and every other individual."[20]

Beauvoir says of this period, "History took hold of me, and never let go thereafter."[21] And certainly events acquired a frightening momentum from this point forward. Hitler and Stalin concluded the non-aggression pact in August 1939, leaving Western Europe open to attack and finally disillusioning Beauvoir completely about the U.S.S.R. Then in September 1939 Hitler marched into Poland, France entered the war, and French troops were mobilized. Sartre went off to join a meteorological unit in the army. Their close friend Jacques Bost, already in the army, could now be called to the front at any time. For those like Beauvoir left in Paris, life was put on hold. In May 1940 Hitler invaded Holland and Belgium. The U.S. still declined to enter the war.

Beauvoir is in the French countryside when the German troops roll in. She is relieved to hear that the army is capitulating because of the French lives it will save, but is shocked by the terms of the Armistice. Sartre becomes a German prisoner of war. Back in occupied Paris she is exposed to German propaganda and is enraged by the extreme policies imposed by the collaborationist Vichy government. She whiles away her enforced leisure reading Hegel's *Phenomenology of Spirit* in the Bibliothèque Nationale. Right-wing intellectuals rush into the vacuum caused by the German victory, filling government posts and taking over the press, all calling for the blood of their enemies.

In March of 1941 Sartre returned to Paris from his prisoner of war camp. There he too had experienced a new sense of solidarity with his fellow humans. He was also filled with a new-found dedication to political action. Fired up by his zeal, Beauvoir threw herself "heart and soul" into a Resistance group made up of students and former fellow students.[22] Lacking the expertise to build or handle weapons, they decided to make contacts, gather information, and put out newsletters and pamphlets. They named their group "Socialism and Liberty" because they also concerned themselves with constructing an agenda for the Left for after the war, although there actually was little ground for believing that Germany would be defeated at this point. The U.S. had yet to enter the war, although the U.S.S.R. had, making life very dangerous for French Communists. Twelve thousand were arrested in June 1941 in Paris alone.[23]

In October Beauvoir agreed with Sartre that "Socialism and Liberty" should be disbanded. Members of related Resistance groups had been arrested and disappeared, never to return again. Sartre and Beauvoir felt they would be responsible for any harm that would come to the others (just as Beauvoir's character Blomart felt he was responsible for the fate of the Resistance members under his command in her novel *The Blood of Others*). Some who see themselves as debunkers of the Sartre and Beauvoir myth have emphasized that the two were never in any personal danger during this period. Certainly their Jewish friends and acquaintances were in much greater danger, a fact that was brought home to Beauvoir when a member of their close circle of friends, a Spanish Jew she called Bourla in her memoirs, was arrested and killed. Yet anyone with any connection to the Resistance who was in the wrong place at the wrong time could end up being arrested. In July 1944 Sartre and Beauvoir had to leave Paris for two months when a member of the *Combat* (newspaper) group named names under torture.

Some writers have condemned specific actions that Beauvoir took during the Occupation. For one, after she lost her teaching job on a morals charge stemming from her relationship with a female student in June 1943, she worked for a German-controlled radio station putting together a show on Medieval history. And before that she signed an oath required of all teachers swearing that she was not a Freemason or a Jew, which Sartre reproached her for when he returned from his prison camp.[24] These facts must be set against the background of her situation, though. She had not only to support herself, but help support some of the close circle of friends who had become economically dependent on her and Sartre. Since she had no other resources to fall back on, she needed a job.

Whether economic hardship excuses these actions can be debated. When dealing with this issue one must keep in mind that people are led to criticize Beauvoir's personal life for a variety of reasons. Those from the other side of the political spectrum look for ways to discredit her. Others are suspicious of all public intellectuals, constantly questioning their fitness to take on such a role. Since Beauvoir worked hard to become a well-known writer, took public political stands, and wrote extensively about her personal life, she set herself up as a target of personal attacks. Even feminists have criticized Beauvoir's life and work in the fifty years since *The Second Sex* was published.

Beauvoir herself writes about "how difficult it was to speak of those days to anyone who had not lived through them."[25] Furthermore, she sometimes seems like her own harshest critic when she writes, for instance, that she feels, "nothing but contempt for this part of my past life."[26] When Sartre returned from his prison camp with a new commitment to political action, she had already realized that her powerlessness was joined to an unshakeable guilt, that "in occupied France the mere fact of being alive implied acquiescence in oppression."[27]

Gradually the tide turned against the Germans. Before the Allied Army arrived in Paris, Parisians made it a point to initiate their own liberation. Beauvoir describes these joyous but fearful days in her memoirs and in a series of articles for the newspaper *Combat*, which were published under Sartre's name.[28] Roaming the streets during these eventful days she felt a bond with everyone she encountered: "All Paris was incarnate in me, and I recognized myself in every face I saw."[29] At this point in her memoirs she sums up the lesson that these years had taught her as follows: "To act in concert with all men, to struggle, to accept death if need be, that life might keep its meaning—by holding fast to these precepts, I felt, I would master that darkness whence the cry of human lamentation arose."[30] It is these precepts that she later laid out and defended in *The Ethics of Ambiguity*.

The years between the moment of liberation and the time that she sat down to compose *The Ethics of Ambiguity* were also momentous. Beauvoir's novel *She Came to Stay*, as well as Sartre's *Being and Nothingness*, were published during the Occupation. *Pyrrhus et Cinéas* was one of the first books published after the Liberation. Beauvoir obviously was an important intellectual figure in her own right. But her renown was increased by her close connection to Sartre. They finally accepted the label of existentialist that had been thrust upon them and now had to defend this new philosophy from its denigrators. That their philosophical stance was a politically engaged one is clear from the introductory essay in the new journal that she and Sartre founded in October 1945, along with Merleau-Ponty,

Raymond Aron, and others. In it Sartre urged writers to write committed literature. This label certainly fits Beauvoir's novel published at the same time, *The Blood of Others*, which depicts the moral dilemmas faced by a band of Resistance fighters. *Les Temps modernes* was not affiliated with any political party. It defended democratic socialism and protested French colonial policies. The day-to-day running of the journal fell mostly to Beauvoir and Merleau-Ponty and she worked very hard at it.

The *Ethics of Ambiguity* was written in early 1946, a time when the political climate seemed very promising to intellectuals on the Left. Eva Lundgren-Gothlin writes: "The period immediately after the war was dominated by a spirit of consensus and general optimism. The shared years of resistance had given rise to a sense of unity which many people hoped would be maintained."[31] An organization of Resistance groups, the Conseil nationale de la Resistance, put together a charter calling for democratic and economic reforms in March 1944, although this agenda was soon deflected. The Communist Party, efficient and organized, had contributed a great deal to the Resistance. Many of its members had been killed or imprisoned by the Germans. Their sacrifices earned the Party a great deal of respect. They were the largest political party in France at the end of the war and part of the government from 1944 to 1947.[32]

Soon after the Liberation the Communist Party began to attack existentialism in the press. One reason was existentialism's philosophical indebtedness to the thought of Heidegger, who had been a member of the Nazi Party and Rector of Freiburg University under Hitler. There were also rumors (which they probably started) that Sartre had been an informer during the war. The real reason for their hostility, however, was the lure that existentialism, which had become wildly popular, exercised on the young, drawing them away from the Party. Chagrined, since he was sympathetic to the Party, Sartre tried to counter their attacks in "Existentialism is a Humanism" and "Materialism and Revolution." Attacks made by Communist writers on her ideas were also one of the reasons Beauvoir was moved to write *The Ethics of Ambiguity*.[33]

At this time, then, neither Beauvoir nor Sartre was a Marxist. Beauvoir's quarrel was strictly with the French Communists of her day, however. Her references to Marx and Trotsky in *The Ethics of Ambiguity* show her respect and affinity for their ideas. Her and

Sartre's distance from the French Communists at this time is shown by the fact that in 1948 they were founding members of the RDR, a left-wing party opposed to Stalin and dedicated to establishing a socialist Europe loyal to neither the U.S. nor the U.S.S.R.

Later in life, perhaps carried along by Sartre's further drift leftward towards communism, Beauvoir adopted a more materialist point of view, which is why in her memoirs she constantly criticizes her earlier ethical essays as being too idealistic. Bringing the concept of the situated subject into play, I have stressed how the position Beauvoir takes in *The Ethics of Ambiguity* must be viewed against the background of her situation at the time. The same is true of her memoirs, of course: they too were written at a specific time and place. *The Prime of Life* was first published in 1960 and *Force of Circumstance* in 1963, while *The Ethics of Ambiguity* was written in 1946.[34] *The Prime of Life* describes the events in her life leading up to and culminating in the liberation of Paris. In *Force of Circumstance*, which covers the postwar period, she deliberately adopts a more pessimistic outlook, because the popularity that *The Prime of Life* enjoyed among the bourgeoisie appalled her. (It particularly galled her when someone called *The Prime of Life* dynamic and optimistic.[35]) In *Force of Circumstance* she wants to impress on the reader that "the truth of the human condition" is that two-thirds of the world's population is hungry.[36] Her new anti-bourgeois, Marxist-tinged materialist stance leads her to call *The Ethics of Ambiguity* the book of hers "that irritates me the most today."[37]

Conclusion

I have offered this account to bring across how Beauvoir's experiences during the war years instilled in her a commitment to political activism. She and many others sat by and did nothing while Fascism swept over Europe and then remained to witness the havoc and atrocities it brought in its wake. The choice as to where to locate herself on the political spectrum seemed clear. Her initial allegiance to the Left was solidified by the way that the Right allied itself with Fascism during these years. Inclined to pacifism at first, she eventually came to realize the necessity of using armed force to stop such a threat. Beauvoir's attitude towards political violence, which some may, and did, condemn, is also understandable given this background. She saw the actions taken by the French Resistance during the war to be morally justified. They were directed against the invading forces of another country, a country engaged in repellant practices such as the deportation and murder of resident Jews.

Of course, in the end Beauvoir's political stance—as well as her philosophical arguments—must be appraised on independent grounds. Historical circumstances do not provide excuses for her. Nonetheless, a familiarity with the historical situation at the time that she wrote her works on ethics can deepen our understanding of them considerably. At the beginning of this chapter I mentioned how the concept of the situated subject informs all of Beauvoir's writing. But she herself *was* a situated subject as well. What she wrote can only be understood fully if this situation is taken into account.

The Works before
The Ethics of Ambiguity

In her memoirs Beauvoir says that her realization in spring 1939 of her connection to others and her subsequent conversion to a more committed political stance marked the beginning of the moral period of her literary career.[1] But in fact until the spring of 1941 Beauvoir was still engaged in finishing what would become her first published novel, *She Came to Stay*. This work does not reflect either a concern with ethics or a politically engaged viewpoint. It depicts a love triangle between three characters who are based on Sartre, Beauvoir and Olga Kosakievicz, a former student of Beauvoir's. The epigraph Beauvoir chose for it is from Hegel's Master/Slave Dialectic: "Each consciousness seeks the death of the other."[2] And it is certainly apt, given that the older female character, Françoise, kills Xavière, the younger female character, at the end. Obviously, Xavière poses a threat to Françoise's relation to Françoise's lover, Pierre. But Beauvoir emphasizes instead the metaphysical threat she represents to Françoise's very subjectivity. As an "alien consciousness," Xavière raises the specter of "death, a total negation, an eternal absence."[3] Beauvoir's description of Françoise's reaction to Xavière bears an uncanny resemblance to Sartre's portrayal of the encounter with the other in *Being and Nothingness*, as commentators have noted.[4]

There is a big difference between Beauvoir's analysis of the relations between subjects in her writings on ethics and the picture of interpersonal relations painted in *She Came to Stay*. Although Beauvoir still thinks that conflicts among individuals inevitably will occur, in *The Ethics of Ambiguity* she argues that some sort of harmony between them is not only possible but necessary for the full flowering of individual freedom. Furthermore these conflicts are seen as having concrete social and political causes, not metaphysical ones. After all, if it is invariably the case that "each consciousness seeks the death of the other," there is not much hope for an ethics.

By the time that Beauvoir finished *She Came to Stay* she recognized that its point of view clashed with her new take on the world. In her memoirs she records how she was already then eager to move on to her new novel about the Resistance, *The Blood of Others*.[5] Apparently, though, Beauvoir's account in her memoirs of when she wrote what during this period is shaped more by a concern for narrative flow than for accuracy. Her biographer Deirdre Bair says that Beauvoir informed her that she actually formulated the ideas for her first philosophical essay, *Pyrrhus et Cinéas,* in early fall 1942, before she began *The Blood of Others*.[6] It was at this same time, Bair speculates, that Beauvoir sketched out the plot for her play *Les Bouches inutiles,* which was not produced until October 1945. (In the memoirs Beauvoir says that she began writing it in spring 1944.) Although it does not matter much what order she wrote them in, I will follow Bair's chronology in discussing these works in this chapter.

Pyrrhus et Cinéas

Pyrrhus et Cinéas was the first of the philosophical essays that Beauvoir wrote in the 1940s. The title refers to two characters in a story related by Plutarch. Michel de Montaigne tells the same story in one of his essays.[7] Beauvoir used a quote from another essay by Montaigne as the epigraph of *The Ethics of Ambiguity*. Indeed the essay form that Beauvoir adopts in *Pyrrhus et Cinéas* traces its lineage back to Montaigne. In the story a great king named Pyrrhus is asked by his advisor Cinéas what he will do after he conquers the land he is setting out for. Why, conquer the next, Pyrrhus replies. And after that? Cinéas continues. Pyrrhus goes on in the same vein. After he has conquered the whole world, Pyrrhus says, he will rest. Cinéas asks, "Why not rest right away?" (PC 9). While Montaigne implies that Cinéas represents the voice of wisdom, Beauvoir holds that, "It is Pyrrhus who is right, and not Cinéas" (PC 60). Beauvoir endorses Pyrrhus's stance towards life, not his desire for military glory. Beauvoir defines human existence here as a constant reaching out for goals. As soon as one goal is accomplished—or dropped—another one is set. Cinéas refuses to grasp this truth, while Pyrrhus does.

The term that Beauvoir uses to describe this defining feature of human existence is transcendence, a term that she also uses in *The Second Sex*. She also says, "man is project," (PC 28) using a term Sartre uses in *Being and Nothingness*. But, whereas Sartre defines the original project to be the choice of a basic attitude towards the world that establishes one's personality, Beauvoir shifts the focus to humans' projects in the plural.[8] Published, as it was, a year after Sartre published *Being and Nothingness*, there is a temptation to see *Pyrrhus et Cinéas* as an extension or a popularization of Sartre's philosophy there. But there are only two references to Sartre in the text, and two more in the notes. And Beauvoir refers to many, many more authors.[9] Although what she says, in the first section of this work at least, harmonizes with what Sartre says in *Being and Nothingness*, that does not mean that *Pyrrhus et Cinéas* does not present Beauvoir's own philosophical views. After all, she says of this period, "I also embraced existentialism for myself."[10]

Pyrrhus et Cinéas is not a work on ethics, at least if ethics is defined in the narrow sense it commonly is today. William McBride points out that existentialism's treatment of "the normative aspects of human existence" has more in common with the broader approach to ethics taken by the ancient Greeks.[11] Beauvoir's subject in *Pyrrhus et Cinéas*—how one should live, or rather, what one should live for—is in this sense ethical.

The work is divided into two parts. In the first part Beauvoir examines a number of answers that have been given to the question: what gives meaning to human life? She shows that each of these answers (the pleasure of the moment, the standpoint of the universe, destiny, God, the concept of mankind, death) does not suffice. Either it negates itself or stands in need of further justification. Take, for instance, those who say that they are here to fulfill God's will on earth. If God is "infinity and fullness of being" (PC 36), then humans can do nothing to add to this. If one appeals instead to a more personal, more human God, then how does one know what his will is? Kierkegaard wrote about this dilemma in *Fear and Trembling*. In choosing how to interpret God's will, one inevitably injects one's own values, or more commonly, those of one's class or historical epoch, Beauvoir points out. She concludes that the only thing that can give meaning to human life is a goal that a person has taken on and given meaning to himself or herself. This first part of *Pyrrhus et Cinéas*, then, indirectly highlights the challenge that existentialism poses for ethics. The only meaning that life has is the meaning that we ourselves give it. It is only our choosing to find a way of life valuable that makes it valuable.

In the second part of *Pyrrhus et Cinéas*, where she analyzes the individual's relation to other people, Beauvoir comes closer to the usual terrain of ethics. There is a right and a wrong stance to take vis-à-vis others, she declares. Her position here on the relation between subjects diverges from Sartre's position in *Being and Nothingness*, as well as from the picture she paints in *She Came to Stay*. Instead of another's freedom threatening to engulf one's own, Beauvoir argues in *Pyrrhus et Cinéas*, one individual's freedom supports and founds another's, like one stone supporting another in an arch.

Beauvoir begins this section with a discussion of another way that people try to give meaning to their lives: they devote themselves to other people. This choice is an ethical stance, although a false one, she judges. It represents the ethics of the dutiful daughter—the *jeune fille rangée* in the title of Beauvoir's subsequent volume of memoirs—that Beauvoir and other women of her class were raised to be. Her explanation for why people adopt this stance looks ahead to her depiction of the woman in love in *The Second Sex*:

> Let's suppose that the other needed me; let's suppose that his existence had an absolute value. Then I am justified in existing since I exist for a being whose existence is justified. I am released from risk, from anguish. In placing an absolute end before me I have given up my freedom. (PC 70)

In *Pyrrhus et Cinéas* Beauvoir is beginning to explore the ways that humans fail to live up to the demands of their freedom—the ways that they fail to achieve moral freedom, in her later terms.

Devoting oneself to others cannot fulfill a person, Beauvoir holds, because one can never do anything *for* another person: "I never create anything for others except points of departure" (PC 79). In explaining why this is so, Beauvoir makes statements that are at odds with her later conception of the relationship between individual freedoms in *The Ethics of Ambiguity*. She says here, "as freedom the other is radically separated from me; no connection can be made between me and this pure interiority upon which even God would have no hold" (PC 88).

Beauvoir's claim in *Pyrrhus et Cinéas* that individuals are radically separate from each other in this way leads her to downplay the impact that violence has on them. For, "if I can do nothing for a man, I can do nothing against him either" (PC 85). Here Beauvoir first introduces her distinction between power and freedom. Violence restricts a person's power, perhaps severely, but it does not touch his or her basic freedom.

Beauvoir realizes the potential implications that her claim that we can do nothing against others has for ethics. She asks, "Is it necessary, then, to conclude that our conduct towards the other does not matter?" Her reply is not very convincing: "Far from it. It does not matter *for him*. . . . But it concerns me, it is *my* conduct, and I am responsible for it" (PC 87). In *The Ethics of Ambiguity* Beauvoir lays out how and why my conduct does matter *for him*. In *Pyrrhus et Cinéas* she can say only why it matters for me.

Perhaps under the influence of Sartre's account in *Being and Nothingness*, or perhaps still under the sway of her own portrayal of dueling freedoms in *She Came to Stay*, Beauvoir characterizes the other's freedom as "dangerous" and "foreign" (PC 105). But dangerous or not, others' freedom provides a foundation for my existence as transcendence: "I need them because once I have gone beyond my own goals, my actions will fall back upon themselves, inert and useless, if they are not carried by new projects towards a new future. . . through other men, my transcendence is always being extended further than the project I am now forming" (PC 110). In sketching out this argument Beauvoir appeals in passing to some of the central themes of *The Ethics of Ambiguity*. She alludes to the *dévoilement* or disclosure of being through subjectivity. She stresses the role that others play in creating the future towards which I am constantly transcending myself. But in the scenario Beauvoir presents in *Pyrrhus et Cinéas* individual freedoms interact with each other only in a leapfrog fashion. To use her metaphor, the individual "is like the leader of an expedition who marks out a new route for his march and who constantly returns to the rear to gather up the stragglers, running forward again to lead his escort further on" (PC 115).

In *Pyrrhus et Cinéas* Beauvoir concludes that in the end violence is bad, not because it harms its victims, but because it harms the perpetrator: "The man to whom I do violence is not my peer, and I need for men to be my peers" (PC 116). In order for others to be my peers their situations must be somehow comparable to mine. Beauvoir does not use this term in this context, but she implies that their situations can be comparable only if they have sufficient power: "I ask for health, knowledge, well-being, leisure, for men so that their freedom is not consumed in fighting sickness, ignorance, misery" (PC 115). (In speaking of a freedom that can be consumed, of course, Beauvoir is going beyond the notion of a freedom of "pure interiority.") I thus have a responsibility to try to provide these things for others.

Les Bouches inutiles

Beauvoir's only play, *Les Bouches inutiles,* published in the U.S. as *Who Shall Die?,* was not a great success when it was produced in October 1945. At the dress rehearsal Beauvoir sat next to Jean Genet, who, she reports, kept muttering, "This isn't what the theater's about! This isn't theater at all."[12] He was right. Didactic and clumsily plotted, it is not a very good play. It does testify to Beauvoir's preoccupation with ethical issues during this period, however. Indeed, that is part of the problem. Beauvoir herself complains that the characters are used merely to represent ethical viewpoints and reports how people thought the dialogue was "too naively inspired by Existentialist philosophy."[13]

The entire play centers on a moral dilemma. In the fourteenth century in the depth of winter the town of Vauxelles in Flanders is fighting for its independence from the Duke of Burgundy. His army has laid siege to the town for an entire year. Food stores are very low. The King of France sends word that he will send armies to free the town in the spring, but there is not enough food to last until then. What should the leaders of the town do?

Their solution is that the old men, the sick, the children, and all the women should be ejected from the town and left, probably, to die. Since food will no longer be wasted on "useless mouths," there will be enough to last until the town is rescued. (Apparently, this practice was actually resorted to in the late Middle Ages. The play was inspired by incidents Beauvoir read about in her historical research.[14] The only other option seems to be surrender, which would be a capitulation to tyranny.

The action of the play, subplots involving various romances aside, centers on overturning this decision. When the option of arming each and every inhabitant and storming the camp of the Burgundian army is presented to the townspeople, they resist it. They object that defeat is certain and that they have no right to sacrifice the town. Louis, a town leader, replies to them in a very existentialist fashion, "Who says what is right but ourselves? The problem which we face now has been solved by no one before, and no one can solve it but ourselves. It is up to us, and to us only, to choose" (WSD 58).

The character of Jean-Pierre is the reluctant hero of the play who comes to recognize the need to forge bonds with others. At first he does not want to engage himself in other people's lives. He rejects Clarice's love and refuses a political role in the town. The way that Beauvoir phrases it is that he wants to keep his hands clean. (The title of Sartre's later play *Dirty Hands*, plays on this same metaphor.) The decision of the town to eject the women, children, old, and sick, which he automatically opposes, shocks him out of this stance. Transformed, he declares his love for Clarice, announcing that one loves on this earth "by joining in a common fight" (WSD 48). Then he exposes a certain town leader as a traitor, takes over his post, and changes the townspeople's minds.

Another theme in *Les Bouches inutiles* is that only by directing one's acts towards the future does one give one's present life meaning. For instance, throughout the play the townspeople, even though hungry and weak, keep toiling away building a bell tower to ring out their eventual victory. There is much talk of thrusting oneself towards the future. "Without this impulse which throws us forwards, we would be no more than a layer of mildew on the face of the earth" (WSD 39), she has one character say.

It is clear why this play belongs to the moral period of Beauvoir's writing career. Although perhaps the least skilled of all of Beauvoir's literary works, it nonetheless contains interesting elements. First, there is the subject of the play. It is ironic that in her memoirs Beauvoir criticizes her writing from this period for ignoring what she identifies there as the most important ethical issue of all: hunger. For that is what this play focuses on—a concrete problem arising from material circumstances—even though its style is rhetoric-laden and artificial. Secondly, the play has a proto-feminist slant to it. It is the women who are to be excluded from the town. When this wrong is righted, the women take up arms beside the men.

The Blood of Others

Beauvoir began writing *The Blood of Others*, which would be her second published novel, in the winter of 1943 and finished the first draft that May.[15] Unlike *Les Bouches inutiles* it is a very well-crafted and complexly-structured work. Like the play, however, it centers on a moral dilemma. The moral dilemma frames a long series of flashbacks that present the important events in the central characters' lives. As the novel begins and ends, Jean Blomart, the leader of a Resistance group, sits beside the bed of his dying lover Hélène. He was the one who sent her on the rescue mission that led to her getting shot and he feels responsible for her fate. By dawn he must decide whether to send other people in the band on a sabotage mission, knowing that (a) they might get killed as well or (b) if they are successful a number of hostages will be shot by the Nazis in reprisal. Existentialism stresses individual responsibility: one must pay for every choice one makes. The question posed by this novel is whether it is right "to pay with the blood of others" (BO 157).

The character of Jean Blomart is a much more fully realized version of the character of Jean-Pierre in *Les Bouches inutiles*. At first, too, his major concern is "not to dirty my hands" (BO 123). Earlier, in rebellion from his middle-class upbringing, he joined the Communist Party, also convincing a young man, the brother of a close friend, to join. The young man gets killed at a demonstration and Blomart leaves the Party, involving himself in the trade union movement instead. As Fascism spreads across Europe his resolve to avoid bloodshed at all costs is gradually undermined, just as Beauvoir's pacifism was. Indeed Beauvoir targets pacifism in the novel. The character who is a committed pacifist is smug and self-righteous and ends up urging "loyal" collaboration with the occupying Germans.[16]

The character of Hélène is very similar to the character of Xavière in *She Came to Stay*. Both are pretty young women who are impulsive, willful, heedless, and completely wrapped up in themselves. (The character of Hélène is based on another of Beauvoir's former students, Natalie Sorokine.) But unlike Xavière, Hélène undergoes a rather amazing transformation over the course of the novel. At the end she serenely accepts dying for others' sake. This change is a gradual one, but perhaps the turning point is when she witnesses policemen tearing Jewish children from their mothers to send them away to the camps. (This scene is probably a reference to *la rafle du Vél d'hiv* in July 1942 in Paris.[17]) When Hélène goes to see Blomart, from whom she is then estranged, to help her Jewish friend escape the Gestapo, she volunteers to work for his Resistance group.

Until this transformation Hélène looks solely to her love for Blomart to justify her existence. Beauvoir uses the character of Hélène to tie this attitude towards love to what existentialism posits as humans' futile desire for being. As Hélène exults when finally Blomart appears to return her love:

> She no longer had a feeling of emptiness inside her, or of uncertainty. She no longer wondered where she should go or what good it was staying there. It was as if there were a special place assigned to her on earth and she exactly fitted into it. (BO 168)

The feeling of emptiness and uncertainty that Hélène attempts to overcome through being loved is her awareness of her lack of being, in the terms Beauvoir uses in *The Ethics of Ambiguity*. Blomart, given to constant philosophical rumination as he is, realizes that Hélène is seeking through his love "a miraculous justification for being what she was" (BO 147). But, he reflects, "how could I justify her existence, I who was here with no reason, with no justification" (BO 185). Only a being whose existence is itself justified could justify another's existence. This is one reason why people turn to religion. Hélène describes her prior belief in God as filling the same need as Blomart's love does: "When I was small, I believed in God, and it was wonderful; at every moment of the day something was required of me; then it seemed to me that I *must* exist" (BO 83).

Another philosophical idea floated in *The Blood of Others* involves the relation between consciousness and the world. When Blomart explains to Hélène why he feels personally responsible for the evil in the world, he alludes to the feeling he has always had that, "my eyes are sufficient for this boulevard to exist; my voice is sufficient for the world to have a voice. When it is silent it's my fault" (BO 146). This theme is not a new one for Beauvoir. At the beginning of *She Came to Stay* she presents an extended meditation on how the existence of things depends on a consciousness perceiving them. As Françoise wanders through the abandoned theater late at night, she reflects:

> When she was not there, the smell of dust, the half-light, the forlorn solitude, all this did not exist for anyone; it did not exist at all. Now that she was there the red of the carpet gleamed through the darkness like a timid night-light. She exercised this power: her presence revived things from their inanimateness; she gave them their color, their smell. She went down one floor and pushed open the door into the auditorium. It was as if she had been entrusted with a mission: she had to bring to life this forsaken theater filled with darkness. . . . She alone released the meaning of these abandoned places, of these slumbering things. She was there and they belonged to her. The world belonged to her.[18]

What Beauvoir is describing in these passages is what she later calls the *dévoilement* or disclosure of being in *The Ethics of Ambiguity*. Only through consciousness is meaning given to the world. That does not mean that consciousness creates the world. As Blomart puts it in *The Blood of Others*, "I didn't create the world, but I create it again, by my presence every instant" (BO 146). In *The Blood of Others* and *She Came to Stay* the focus is on how an individual consciousness anchors the world. In *The Ethics of Ambiguity*, it is on how humans disclose the world together.

In *The Blood of Others* Blomart ruminates on how the world is rooted in consciousness in this way as he watches Hélène die. This scene is most likely drawn from Beauvoir's experience of sitting by her father's deathbed.[19] As Hélène dies, Blomart reflects, "the world dematerializes . . . the future is telescoped into the stationary moment; soon . . . there will be no world" (BO 80). At the moment of Hélène's death what Beauvoir calls in *The Ethics of Ambiguity* the ambiguity of the human condition—humans' dual existence as consciousness and material entity—is brought vividly home to Blomart: "She breathes once more, the eyes cloud over; the world detaches itself from her, it crumbles; and yet she does not slide out of the world; it is in the heart of the world that she becomes the dead woman that I hold in my arms" (BO 290). After death, something is gone, but something remains and both what is gone and what remains made up the living human being.

The Blood of Others also places an emphasis on human freedom, which is the touchstone of Beauvoir's ethics. Beauvoir concludes the novel with a paean to freedom, calling it "the supreme good" and "that good which saves each man from all the others and from myself" (BO 292). (In chapter 5 I discuss why it is problematic to define freedom as a good in this way.) Blomart appeals to this supreme good to justify his ultimate decision to send off the Resistance fighters under his command on a new mission. Freedom is the ethical ideal in this novel, as in *The Ethics of Ambiguity*, that justifies spilling the blood of others.

However, freedom is conceived quite differently in *The Blood of Others* than in *The Ethics of Ambiguity*. Blomart complains in the novel that we can never "touch" the freedom of the other: "I can only get as far as his outward actions, and to him I am nothing more than an outer appearance" (BO 127). This freedom that Blomart is talking about in *The Blood of Others* is the freedom of interiority that Beauvoir describes in *Pyrrhus et Cinéas*. The way that freedom is represented in *The Blood of Others* can even be seen as a step backwards from the way she conceives it in *Pyrrhus et Cinéas*. In *Pyrrhus et Cinéas* Beauvoir uses the image of individual freedoms supporting each other like stones in an arch. In *The Blood of Others*, instead of stones in an arch, other people's freedom becomes a stumbling block. "You stumbled against me as you stumbled against a stone" (BO 288–89), Blomart tells Hélène when he is coming to grips with his feelings of responsibility for her death.

But does what Blomart says on the subject of freedom in the novel really represent Beauvoir's view of it? In her later collection of short stories *The Woman Destroyed* Beauvoir uses the literary convention of the unreliable narrator. The three central female characters complain about their lot, but the reader is supposed to realize that they themselves are to blame. Blomart is the main voice speaking in *The Blood of Others*. Are we to accept everything *he* says? It is obvious that Hélène undergoes a transformation over the course of the novel. What is not so obvious is that Blomart changes his basic outlook as well. Throughout the novel he feels responsible for what happens to everyone with whom he has come into contact. He feels especially that he is responsible for Hélène's death. But in the closing pages of the novel, Hélène insists that he is not, *she* is, because she herself made the choice to risk her life. When this dawns on Blomart: "the vice about his heart was loosened, and hope rose in the night" (BO 288).[20] In this scene Beauvoir implies that Blomart's previous grasp of the moral consequences of his freedom was one-sided. He is free and thus responsible for his actions, but so is everyone else free and thus responsible for their actions. Blomart's new perspective at the end of the novel seems to subvert the statement by Dostoevsky that serves as its epigraph: "Each of us is responsible for everything and to each human being."

The Blood of Others is a novel that champions human freedom, but this somewhat ambiguous ending leaves up in the air what human freedom entails. Does our freedom make us each a stumbling block in others' way? What exactly is each of us responsible for? The novel leaves no doubt that each individual's freedom has an impact on many other people. But this is no reason, Beauvoir seems to be saying, to shun political engagement. In the novel freedom is a burden, although perhaps not quite so much of a burden as Blomart first envisions it to be. Only later in *The Ethics of Ambiguity* does Beauvoir provide a rationale for taking up this burden.

The *Temps modernes* Articles

From November 1945 to April 1946 Beauvoir published four philosophical essays in *Les Temps modernes*, the new journal she and Sartre had just started. Discounted by Beauvoir, they have been largely ignored by commentators. One, "Littérature et metaphysique," on the subject of the metaphysical novel, gives an indication of what Beauvoir tried to achieve in her own fiction. But it is the other three on existentialism and ethics that I will discuss here, because in them one can see the beginnings of Beauvoir's existentialist ethics. Since their importance has been overlooked, I will go into them at some length.

"Idéalisme morale et réalisme politique"

In the first essay published in November 1945 Beauvoir describes what she calls an authentic morality. To talk of an authentic morality represents a big step forward from Sartre's *Being and Nothingness*, published in 1943, which only hints at the possibility of overcoming bad faith and achieving authenticity. Beauvoir's description of an authentic morality is not the centerpiece of the essay, however. It arises in the context of another issue: the conflict between the two opposed attitudes of moral idealism and political realism that people take towards politics. Unlike in the past, she says: "At present almost everyone has a political existence" (IMRP 50). When she wrote these words, of course, the French had just lived through a period when they were faced with making political decisions on an almost daily basis: whether to collaborate with the Germans, whether to aid or join the Resistance, and so on.

Beauvoir uncovers the metaphysical assumptions behind the attitude of political realism and rejects them. Basically, those who adopt this attitude make the same mistake that the personality type she later calls the serious man does. (She also accuses those who take this attitude of "bad faith" [IMRP 69].) They assume that the ends that they pursue are objectively given, that they are "inscribed in reality," and justified by objective values that reside "on the plane of being" (IMRP 57, 62). They fail to recognize that all ends are set up as ends by human freedom. Historical leaders (including Charles V, who will figure prominently in her next novel) who seek the glory of France or the Empire make this error. Those who do not lead but choose instead to see themselves merely as swept along by "the great current of history" (IMRP 61) fall prey to another illusion. Many French people, for instance, justified their collaboration with the Germans by saying that they did not believe that Hitler could be defeated. But, she notes, if everyone had taken this attitude, Hitler never *would* have been defeated.

Political realists are found on both sides of the political spectrum. Beauvoir reserves her greatest scorn for those bourgeois who argue that their economic dominance is both justified and inevitable. They see their class as upholding certain unquestioned spiritual values against the sordid materialism of the working class. It is thus right that they enjoy the fruits of capitalism, because they use them for higher ends. Their spiritual superiority also justifies them in dictating the conditions of the workers' lives. Even those enlightened members of the bourgeoisie who want to improve the living conditions of the working class get it wrong according to Beauvoir. They fail to see that "the good of man is not something that can be given to him from the outside" (IMRP 69).

Beauvoir's critique of conservatism leads her into a short discussion of economic oppression. As in *The Ethics of Ambiguity* Beauvoir sees its worst consequence to be that "a man who seeks only to keep himself alive does not have a political existence" (IMRP 66). In her memoirs Beauvoir criticized these essays: "Why did I write concrete liberty instead of bread . . . I never brought matters down to saying: People must eat because they are hungry."[21] Here she rejects a purely materialist analysis of oppression in words that could serve as a rebuttal to her subsequent criticism. Bread is not simply bread, she writes: "it is also life, the right to live for oneself and for others, in the present as well as in the future" (IMRP 67). The important thing is not just to end hunger. What is important is that the workers themselves seek a new level of existence and define its significance. Why are workers willing to risk their lives to change their situation, if just remaining alive is their only goal, she asks. What they want is not just to survive, but instead "the affirmation of their ability to improve their lot themselves" (IMRP 67).

Political realists on the Left, by comparison, say they recognize that it is more important for people to have freedom than material goods. The mistake they make is to assume that the end that they seek—for example, political revolution or economic liberation—justifies using any means necessary to attain it. Beauvoir's target here, as in her treatment of this theme in *The Ethics of Ambiguity*, is the French Communist Party and other Stalinists of this era. (Keep in mind that the Hitler-Stalin Pact had been signed only six years previously.) Beauvoir is no Kantian. She admits that "it is impossible to act for mankind without treating certain men, at certain instants, as means" (IMRP 82-83). Nonetheless, she argues here and in *The Ethics of Ambiguity* that certain means are ruled out, not on abstract moral grounds, but because they contradict the end aimed at: "A victory obtained by renouncing the ideal one is defending is the worst of defeats" (IMRP 71). In the end political realists on the Left make the same metaphysical error that those on the Right do. They see the end that they pursue as something given and fixed, with an objective value.

Beauvoir's rejection of the stance of moral idealism is, if anything, more vehement. But to reject this stance is to reject a certain type of morality, not morality as a whole. Beauvoir identifies moral idealism with traditional, classical morality, a more or less adulterated Kantianism that appeals to universal imperatives and worships justice, right, and truth as "great idols enshrined in an intelligible heaven" (IMRP

52). A person engaged in politics cannot live up to these standards, so
the virtuous soul withdraws from it and confines himself or herself to
making symbolic gestures. Beauvoir makes her most pointed criticism
of Kant in this essay: it is impossible to deduce what one should do in
an actual situation from an abstract universal law, she says. Many people intuit these shortcomings of traditional morality. That is why, even
though they give lip service to it in public, they turn away from it in
practice. Ethics thus becomes "a ceremonious gratuitous game
reserved for a few specialists" (IMRP 55). Those who actually act in
the world are cut off from any moral foundation and the public is
seized by a "profound malaise" (IMRP 81).

Beauvoir wants to replace this bankrupt form of morality with an
authentic morality. Authentic morality does not appeal to a collection
of already constituted values and principles as traditional morality
does. Rather it is the constituting of values and principles. Beauvoir
strikes a Nietzschean note here: "The great moralists were not virtuous souls docilely submitting to a pre-established code of good and
evil" (IMRP 78). An authentically moral act "carries its justification
within itself" (IMRP 79). It is a type of realism. But an authentically
moral person does not tailor his or her actions to fit a pre-given reality. Rather he or she attempts to create a reality that reflects human
aspirations. This person does not shun politics, as the moral idealist
does. Authentic morality is political through and through. However,
since an act carries its justification within itself, the end does not justify the means, as the political realist claims.

What Beauvoir describes as an authentic morality transcends and
reconciles the two opposed positions of moral idealism and political
realism. Was this opposition that she sets up designed from the start
to lead to this Hegelian synthesis? It is not clear. What is clear is that
in this essay Beauvoir has progressed from taking positions on ethical
issues, as in *The Blood of Others* and *Les Bouches inutiles*, to actually
identifying a type of ethics that she advocates. It will fall to *The Ethics
of Ambiguity* to describe this authentic form of morality at greater
length and provide a philosophical foundation for it.

"L'Existentialisme et la sagesse des nations"

In the essay published in the next issue of *Les Temps modernes*
Beauvoir turns from advocating an authentic morality to defending
existentialism. Only later in *The Ethics of Ambiguity* does she join

these two themes together by identifying an authentic ethics *as* an existentialist ethics. In this essay she publically accepts for the first time the label of existentialist that had been thrust on her and Sartre (for the sake of simplicity, she says).

The charges that Beauvoir wants to defend existentialism from are revealing. She denies it is "a doctrine that repudiates friendship, fraternity and all forms of love; [that] it encloses the individual in an egoistic solitude; [that] it cuts away the real world and immures the individual in a fortress of pure subjectivity" (ESN 13–14). Beauvoir obviously does not think that existentialism rules out the possibility of humans forming meaningful bonds with each other. The question, of course, is what she means by existentialism here. Sartre's analysis of being-for-others in *Being and Nothingness*, with its contention that love always reverts to sadism or masochism, does not hold out much hope for positive human relations. Instead of defending Sartre's existentialism from this charge, Beauvoir is (without announcing it) sketching out her own version of existentialism. She says that "the existentialists are so far from denying love, friendship, fraternity that in their eyes it is only in human relations that each individual can find the foundation and accomplishment of his being" (ESN 37). This claim only makes sense in the context of Beauvoir's later argument in *The Ethics of Ambiguity* that individuals find genuine freedom through engaging in joint projects with others. Obviously Beauvoir must include herself among "the existentialists" she is talking about.

Instead of providing a positive characterization of existentialism, however, Beauvoir goes on the offensive, attacking the assumptions of those who attack existentialism. She deftly dissects the underlying view of the world that these people subscribe to. This is the "wisdom of nations" her title refers to, the worldly wisdom of the man of the world who has had long experience of human folly. (The phrase "wisdom of nations" is misleading. It has nothing to do with international politics.) People like this are willing to parrot traditional pieties about virtue when the occasion calls for it, but underneath they know that humans are brutish creatures ruled only by appetite. When people act their worst, they shrug and say, "it's only human." Even the greatest heroes are plagued by human weaknesses, they like to point out.

Sartre famously claimed that existentialism *is* a humanism, but both Sartre and Beauvoir rejected a particular type of humanism. The pessimistic humanism that Beauvoir critiques here is the flip side of the humanism of the Renaissance, which elevated humans almost to the level of gods. Pessimistic humanism constantly reminds us that "human nature will never change" (ESN 20). For existentialism, of course, there is no such thing as human nature and humans *can* change themselves and the societies they live in. The philosophical basis of pessimistic humanism is a type of psychological egoism that holds that everyone acts in his or her self-interest. Thus people are forever separated from one another, because their interests inevitably conflict. The picture of human existence painted by existentialism is nowhere near so grim and gloomy. It is this worldly wisdom that denies that true love or true friendship is possible, not existentialism, Beauvoir charges.

This attitude appeals to people because it excuses their own lapses. But they feel no need to hold to it always. They find the demands for logical consistency and moral coherence made by existentialism, by contrast, burdensome. The determinism underlying this psychology of self-interest also saves people from making any effort to improve people's lives. After all, they ask, what can you expect from such creatures? Beauvoir says, "People like to think that virtue is easy. . . . They resign themselves also without a lot of pain to accepting that virtue is impossible. But what they are loathe to accept is that it is both possible and difficult" (ESN 39). Existentialism upsets people because it places a moral demand on them. Beauvoir in this essay sees existentialism not as a philosophy that can have an ethics appended to it, as many commentators have taken Sartre's brief remarks about ethics in *Being and Nothingness* to mean, but rather as a philosophy that implies an ethical stance from the beginning.

Beauvoir's own philosophical perspective informs the comparisons that she makes between existentialism and this worldly philosophy. An egoism like this rests on a false view of subjectivity, she says. It regards the experiencing subject as an object in the world with certain properties, for instance, interests and drives and needs. Using terminology that she relies on extensively in *The Second Sex*, Beauvoir characterizes this view of the world as a philosophy of immanence. Existentialism, on the other hand, is a philosophy of transcendence. According to it the subject is nothing like an object in the world; indeed the subject does not exist except as an originating point for action. Only because it does not exist can it have a desire for being, a desire that motivates much human behavior, as Beauvoir emphasizes in her novels.

Another way to express this insight, Beauvoir says, is to say that existentialism identifies subjectivity and freedom: it defines man as freedom. This identification of subjectivity with freedom (ontological freedom) is the first principle of Beauvoir's existentialism and the starting point of her argument in *The Ethics of Ambiguity*. As a philosophy of freedom existentialism is a paradigmatically optimistic philosophy. But as a philosophy of freedom it makes moral demands on one. This feature of existentialism is what really disturbs its critics, not its pessimism, she concludes.

"Oeil pour oeil"

In her memoirs Beauvoir characterizes these *Temps modernes* articles as pieces she dashed off in response to concerns of the moment, which completely covers over their philosophical significance, both generally and in terms of her intellectual development. Unlike the others, however, the next essay published in February 1946 really was an occasional piece. The occasion was the war crimes trial of the French writer Robert Brasillach, which Beauvoir attended. Brasillach was a committed Fascist and anti-Semite who edited the collaborationist journal *Je Suis Partout* during the Occupation. After he was convicted and sentenced to death Beauvoir was asked to sign a petition requesting clemency for him. She refused, although many noted French intellectuals, such as Albert Camus, did sign.[22] In this essay Beauvoir argues that Brasillach's execution was justified.

In the tradition of Hannah Arendt's *Eichmann in Jerusalem*, however, this essay is more philosophy than journalism.[23] It deserves sustained analysis because it appeals to certain concepts that went on to be central to Beauvoir's ethics. For one, Beauvoir's thesis about the ambiguity of human existence, which she leads off *The Ethics of Ambiguity* with, first surfaces here. In this essay she defines "the ambiguity of man's condition" as lying in his being "at the same time a freedom and a thing, united and dispersed, isolated by his subjectivity but nevertheless coexisting at the heart of the world with other men" (OPO 140).

Beauvoir uses this first aspect of human ambiguity as the basis of her argument that vengeance against people like Brasillach is justified. What makes humans human is their ambiguous nature as material entity and consciousness, and to fail to recognize this aspect of their

existence, or worse, to try to suppress it, is to commit a wrong against
their very humanity. There is such a thing as absolute evil, Beauvoir
says; it is "when someone deliberately tries to degrade a man by
reducing him to a thing" (OPO 135–36). How does one reduce
another human being to a thing? Beauvoir mentions torture, humili-
ation, servitude, assassination. The prime example of course is how
the Nazis treated the Jews, especially in the concentration camps. By
denouncing Jews and revealing their whereabouts in his newspaper,
Brasillach was directly responsible for a number of people suffering
this fate.[24] Beauvoir argues that because their intent was to deny their
victims their humanity, the crimes of the Nazis and their French collaborators were different from ordinary civil crimes, which are motivated by social factors like poverty.

The crimes committed by the Nazis and their henchmen had a
metaphysical dimension, Beauvoir claims. In cases like these the one
in power arrogates to himself one aspect of human existence, freedom
and subjectivity, and consigns to his victim the other, mere material
existence. Only if one recognizes that humans possess this dual nature
as thing and consciousness, is doing this truly wrong. If human beings
are purely material entities, as materialists claim, there is nothing
intrinsically wrong with treating them like things, for they are things
to start with. There might be other reasons for not allowing such
treatment (for example, if it leads to social disharmony). But treating
humans as things would not violate what it means to be human.

The ambiguity of human existence is the basis of a reciprocity
between human beings, Beauvoir goes on to assert. Each human
being shares this feature of human existence with all other human
beings. This reciprocity entails a moral obligation not to treat others
in such a way as to deny the dual nature of their existence. A person
must recognize that "the respect he demands for himself, each person
claims for his fellows and finally for all humans" (OPO 116). This reciprocity is "the metaphysical basis of the idea of justice" (OPO 116).
To fail to treat others this way is always an injustice.

Vengeance is morally justified for Beauvoir in response to such
crimes because it attempts to restore the reciprocity that these crimes
negate. Treating the victimizer like a thing himself can make him realize that he is a material entity too, just as his victim was. If it is his former victim who turns the tables on him in this way, as it is in cases
where vengeance is "pure," Beauvoir holds, then he must recognize

something else he denied: that his former victim is a free subjectivity just like him. He becomes aware of his bond with his victim, which is the ambiguous existence they both share.

Beauvoir realizes that the goal of vengeance is hardly if ever achieved. There are practical reasons why private vengeance, the type that Beauvoir thinks has the greatest chance of concretely reestablishing human reciprocity, should not be allowed. For one, it sometimes leads to the death or suffering of innocent people. But vengeance is also liable to fail to achieve the goal that Beauvoir assigns it because of the very nature of human freedom. The moral goal of all punishment is not just to make wrongdoers suffer, but to make them suffer for what they have done. But in order for this goal to be fulfilled, they themselves must realize that they are suffering for what they have done. If not, then their punishment seems like an act of fate. They react to it the way they would react to a natural disaster. For Beauvoir the goal of vengeance is to get the victimizer to feel what he previously ignored, his own existence as a material being and his victim's free subjectivity. But he must choose to recognize this reciprocity himself; he cannot be forced to do so. As long as he is alive and still capable of thought, he is still free to reject this insight. If, on the other hand, his subjectivity is engulfed by his suffering through the use of force, then vengeance misses its aim, because he can no longer reflect on the meaning of his punishment.

Yet the fact that vengeance is unlikely to achieve its goal is no reason to give up on punishing people who commit acts like these, Beauvoir says. For existentialism all human enterprises, especially those inspired by an authentic morality, are dogged by failure: "like hatred and vengeance, love and action always imply failure, but this failure does not keep us from loving and acting" (OPO 140). We cannot let such crimes go unpunished because, as Beauvoir argues in *The Ethics of Ambiguity*, we have a moral obligation to honor the freedom of those whom they victimize.

All Men Are Mortal

Beauvoir finished writing *All Men Are Mortal*, her next novel, at the end of 1945, right before she began *The Ethics of Ambiguity*. It has two separate plot lines centering on the two main characters, with the first plot framing the second. In the first, Regina, a renowned actress in 1940s France, becomes involved with a man who hundreds of years earlier drank a potion that made him immortal. This encounter transforms her life. Embedded in this story is the much longer account of the experiences of this man, Raymond Fosca, throughout more than 600 years of history. This fantastical touch sets off this novel from the rest of Beauvoir's fiction, which stays within the boundaries of psychological realism.

The scope of this novel is also larger than that of her other novels. Indeed, looking back one can see how the scope of her novels has progressively widened up to this point. *She Came to Stay* focuses on the personal lives of a small group of self-absorbed individuals. The fact that their relationships play themselves out against the backdrop of World War II is almost incidental. In *The Blood of Others*, by comparison, the rise of Fascism and the triumph of the Nazis raise important moral issues for the characters, issues they try to evade but ultimately cannot. *All Men Are Mortal*, on the other hand, transcends any particular historical context. The novel's focus is not the impact of history on any one individual, but rather the individual's relation to history as such. Individual relationships, so important in *She Came to Stay*, shrink into insignificance by the end.

The first plot, the one that centers on Regina, is reminiscent of *She Came to Stay* in that Beauvoir uses interpersonal relations to make metaphysical points about human subjectivity. The same theme that is introduced in *She Came to Stay* and briefly highlighted in *The Blood of Others* is touched on here: how objects need "someone to look at them to make them spring to life" (AMM 39). Regina's apartment, like the empty theater in *She Came to Stay*, is described as requiring a human presence in order for its contents to exist. But through the character of Regina Beauvoir takes this theme one step further. Regina feels that she needs others to look at her in order for *her* to exist. It is thus significant that she is an actress. Only when many eyes are trained on her can she really believe in her existence. When she is not performing she likes to look at herself in the mirror, reflecting how good it would be if there were two of her, "one who lived and the other who watched" (AMM 5). Regina is perhaps the most unpleasant female character in all of Beauvoir's fiction (which is saying something). Clearly she is a person who lives in bad faith, to use Sartre's term. However, Regina's desire to have others look at her does not jibe with Sartre's description of being-for-others in *Being and Nothingness,* where to be looked at by another leads to shame and alienation. Regina's inauthenticity in this novel seems to lie in her desire for being. She, as well as other characters in the novel, are recurrently described as "trying to exist" (AMM 49).

It is Regina's unquenchable desire to exist for others that gets her embroiled with Fosca. She is piqued by the fact that he lies in the courtyard of the hotel she is staying at day after day completely oblivious to everything and, most importantly, to her. So she inserts herself into his life. When Fosca reveals his immortality to her Regina sees him as her means to achieve existence or the state of being once and for all. No longer will she have to depend on an ever-changing cast of spectators. If she exists in his eyes, since he will live forever and remember her, she will exist forever. But Regina is cruelly mistaken. So many people and places have existed for Fosca over the more than 600 years he has been alive, that nothing can have more than a momentary significance for him. Gradually she comes to realize that the point of view that Fosca's immortality imposes on him, a point of view that swallows up her own, is a "curse." The curse is to see the world as "nothing but a parade of fleeting images" (AMM 53). In Fosca's eyes she herself is nothing more than a fleeting image. Through this encounter she realizes that her existence has no more significance than that of a blade of grass.

This revelation shatters Regina's life. The breaking point comes during a party that she throws. It is a great success, but Fosca's presence there makes it into a sham. As she sees him looking at it the room is transformed into a stage set peopled by mannequins wearing masks. What has given Regina's life meaning before, made her exist—the fact that she was always an actress playing to an appreciative audience—now makes her life a lie and a game: "The game of mistress of the house, the game of glory, the game of seduction—all of them were only one single game, the game of existence" (AMM 63). Trying to break free from this game, she announces the end of her acting career and then starts smashing furnishings. Fosca leaves, but she traces him down and makes him tell her the story of his very long life.

The second plot line follows Fosca's life from his birth in the fictitious town of Carmona, Italy in 1279 up to the point that he meets Regina. The central irony of his story is that immortality, which humans have always yearned for, turns out to be something nobody would want. Beauvoir's point is that it is only because humans do die that their lives have any meaning. The limitations of human life are what redeem it. In *Pyrrhus et Cinéas* Beauvoir repeats the advice of Voltaire's Candide that we should cultivate our gardens. But this advice is not much use, she continues, for how do we know how far our garden stretches? As his life runs on and on, Fosca keeps enlarging his garden, yet no matter how large it becomes, he still finds no fulfillment in it. After arranging to become an advisor to the Hapsburg emperor Charles V, he finds that even the whole of Europe is not large enough. So Fosca sets sail for the New World, to survey Charles's territories, where he encounters only ruin and misery. As he looks at the empty sea, the futility of his ambition begins to dawn on him. He reflects: "What, after all, *is* the world? *Where* is it?" (AMM 188).

Fosca looks to many of the same things to give meaning to his life that Beauvoir lists in *Pyrrhus et Cinéas*, but eventually rejects each of them. What he eventually learns is what Beauvoir has already argued in *Pyrrhus et Cinéas* and "Idéalisme morale et réalisme politique": one can never do anything *for* another person. The people whom he loves and devotes himself to all come to resent him. They and the faceless multitudes he aims to help do not want happiness brought to them: "It's not happiness they want; they want to live. . . . It's never what they receive that has value in their eyes; it's what they do" (AMM 202).

Beauvoir uses the character of Fosca to get across the point that from the standpoint of eternity human life and human history have no meaning. There is a positive message in the novel as well, although it tends to get engulfed by Fosca's world-weary cynicism, since the story is told mostly in his voice. To grasp it one must keep in mind that no actual human being can take the standpoint of eternity. Beauvoir does hold out the prospect that a mortal human being can find meaning in life, by contrast. This message is conveyed through the character of Armand, a descendant of Fosca's who fights for the liberation of the workers in the 1848 Revolution.

Armand is a positive figure because he accepts and affirms the limitations of human life, something that Fosca obviously cannot do. Armand declares: "A limited future, a limited life—that's our lot as men. And it is enough" (AMM 328). Beauvoir has Armand contest the claim of another character, Garnier, who leads his troops to certain death even though the cause is lost, that "we don't have to count on the future to give a meaning to our acts" (AMM 312). Armand asserts instead that the future does give meaning to our acts, but that "we should concern ourselves only with that part of the future on which we have a hold" (AMM 328). We act for a limited future, Armand recognizes, and we can expect only a limited success. Celebrating their victory in the streets of Paris, Armand reminds Fosca, "Tomorrow we will have to fight again" (AMM 338). (A prophetic statement: four years later Napoleon III overthrew the Second Republic.) Only within the context of such limitations can there be anything like victory, Fosca finally realizes. Armand wants to be free and hears the voices of others clamoring to be free. What makes him want freedom for himself and others is the joy that he takes in living: "I like to see the sun shining . . . I like rivers and the sea. How can anyone sit back and allow those magnificent forces that are in man to be choked off?" (AMM 319).

Armand is also the source of another important realization for Fosca. When Fosca shares with him his hard-earned insight that one can never do anything *for* another person, Armand replies that he is one of the people he is fighting for; they are fighting together. Fosca realizes that the problem all along has been that he has never been part of humanity. He cannot have at stake what other people have at stake: "Because I wanted nothing for myself *with* them, there was nothing I could want *for* them" (AMM 333).

This realization of Fosca's shows that *All Men Are Mortal* represents a turning point in Beauvoir's conception of the relation individual freedoms are able to forge with one another. In *Pyrrhus et Cinéas* when she argues that we can never do anything *for* others, she does not consider whether we can do anything *with* them. In *Pyrrhus et Cinéas* she takes the disengaged perspective of a Fosca; she had not yet broken through to the perspective of Armand. In *All Men Are Mortal* the bonds that humans can form are brought into relief because they are intuited by someone who, precisely because he lacks the limitations that define the human condition, can never form them himself. Only in *The Ethics of Ambiguity*, though, does this idea of the individual working with people to pursue common goals take center stage. There such activity becomes the hallmark of an authentic realization of freedom: moral freedom.

Looking Ahead to *The Ethics of Ambiguity*

Beauvoir finished *All Men Are Mortal* on her ski holiday at the end of 1945. In February 1946 she began the work that would become *The Ethics of Ambiguity*, encouraged by the response she had received to *Pyrrhus et Cinéas* and her essays in *Les Temps modernes*.[25] She originally conceived the idea for it, she said, in a discussion with one of Sartre's students after she gave a lecture in February 1945 where he defended her from a hostile audience of Gabriel Marcel's Catholic students.[26] Sartre was in the United States visiting his lover Dolorès until he returned to Paris on March 15 and promptly took to bed with the mumps. In her memoirs she includes many diary entries from this period where she records the intense effort she put into writing the work and the exhilaration and exasperation it brought her. She finished it in May right before she and Sartre left on a trip to Switzerland. It was first published in two installments in *Les Temps modernes* in January and February 1947 and then by Gallimard in November 1947 as a small book.[27]

I analyze this work closely in the next chapter. At this point I want only to mention how the themes that I have traced out in her writings prior to *The Ethics of Ambiguity* look ahead to this work. First, Beauvoir's conception of subjectivity, which she identifies with freedom and which she holds is always connected to the world, informs all these previous works. She even describes in her novels how, in one sense, the world is brought into existence by consciousness. But a human being is not just a consciousness. In "Oeil pour oeil" Beauvoir stresses how humans have a material side to their existence too. Beauvoir refers to this two-sided nature of human existence as their ambiguity. This concept serves as the ontological foundation of her existentialist ethics in *The Ethics of Ambiguity*. In these writings she also refers to how people look to the future to give meaning to their lives and shows how humans' desire for being, expressed most strongly in her female characters' attitude towards love, leads to inauthentic behavior.

The central theme of *The Ethics of Ambiguity* is the necessary interrelationship of human freedoms. Even though in *Pyrrhus et Cinéas* she still conceives of freedom as a freedom of interiority, she argues there that it needs to have other freedoms present to give it content. Freedom is greatly valorized in *The Blood of Others*, but it is not entirely clear what freedom involves. Although freedom is hardly mentioned in *All Men Are Mortal*, Beauvoir makes a breakthrough in this novel when she has Fosca discover through the character of Armand how working *with*, not *for* others, can give human life meaning, even though no preset goal can. What still remains is for her to work out the philosophical basis of her ideas about freedom in *The Ethics of Ambiguity* in the context of her own version of existentialism.

4

Willing Others Free:
The Ethics of Ambiguity

The Ethics of Ambiguity has three parts. The first part, "Ambiguity and Freedom," is the shortest and most densely written. In it Beauvoir ponders the sort of being humans have and the consequences this has for ethics. A discussion of existentialism then leads to an analysis of freedom. The second section, "Personal Freedom and Others," describes five different personality types that represent different attitudes that people take towards their freedom. In what follows I analyze these sections closely. Then I turn to what I take to be Beauvoir's main thesis in *The Ethics of Ambiguity*: in order to be genuinely free a person needs to interact with others who are working to develop genuine freedom. I discuss the third section of the book, "The Positive Aspect of Morality," mostly in the next two chapters. There, Beauvoir surveys the difficulties that arise in making ethical decisions in concrete situations.

Ambiguity

The ancient Athenians believed that their forebears sprang directly from the earth rather than being created by gods or born of human parents. In some versions of the myth, the ancestor was depicted as having a man's form above the waist and a snake's form below: "Having emerged from the earth, he still in part resembled the creature that slips to and fro between the upper and lower worlds."[1] At the beginning of *The Ethics of Ambiguity*, Beauvoir asserts that there is a fundamental ambiguity to human life. According to her, every human, like the chthonic ancestor of the Athenians, exists at the same time in two realms: "he is still part of the world of which he is a consciousness" (EA 7, my translation). Rooted as they are in the earth, humans can transcend their material origin in thought, but they can never escape it.

Beauvoir also refers to this fundamental ambiguity in her earlier philosophical essays. In "Idéalisme moral et réalisme politique" she mentions how the ancient Greeks believed that they were denizens of two realms: the polis and a realm of subterranean powers.[2] In "Oeil pour oeil" she uses this concept in her condemnation of the crimes of the Nazis. By denying human ambiguity in treating people like things, they violated their humanity. In *The Ethics of Ambiguity* this concept serves as the foundation of her ethics.

Here she cites many ways that this ambiguity is manifested in human life. Humans live and they die. They can retreat to an internal realm of consciousness free from external restraints, but they always exist as bodies, as things "crushed by the dark weight of other things" (EA 7). They can discover seemingly eternal truths, including the truth of their own ambiguity, but they are always tied to the fleeting moment of the present. Each is a unique individual immersed in the collective whole of humanity.

Most philosophers try to escape the tension that accepting this basic ambiguity entails by constructing systems that privilege one of a pair of opposed terms, she says. In the modern Western tradition the prevalent distinction is between mind and matter, or the corollary distinction between mind and body. Materialist philosophers attempt to reduce one side of this pair, mind, to the other, matter. Idealists of different stripes attempt the opposite. Dualists settle instead for a permanent standoff with both co-existing in the individual human being, in Francis Jeanson's words, "like eternal strangers."[3] "Spirit" and "Nature" are the names that Hegel gives to the two opposing poles. More ingeniously, he attempts "to reject none of the aspects of man's condition and to reconcile all of them." But Beauvoir repudiates Hegel's "marvelous optimism" (EA 8). Siding instead with Kierkegaard, she characterizes the ambiguity of the human condition as tragic. Like the conflicts at the heart of Greek tragedy, it cannot be overcome but must be played through to the end.

Why can it not be overcome? Beauvoir gives no argument. Rather she implies that there is a relation of dependence existing between the poles. She says of the human being: "In turn an object for others, he is nothing more that an individual in the collectivity on which he depends" (EA 7). The individual is dependent on the human community for its birth and sustenance. There is an "original helplessness from which man surges up" (EA 12). Likewise, the existence of consciousness is dependent on the human body and its continuing functioning. For this reason death, Beauvoir stresses, is inevitable and indeed possible at any moment. And because consciousness is interwoven with the body a human subject can become an object for another human subject.[4] Finally, without consciousness there can be no revelation of enduring truths. But consciousness depends on the body, which exists in time, not in an atemporal realm.[5]

The ambiguity of the human condition cannot be overcome because of this dependence of consciousness on the body and the self on others. However, materialist philosophers, given that they accept the distinct existence of consciousness at all, would readily endorse the conclusion that consciousness is dependent on something material (as epiphenomenalists, for instance, assert). Beauvoir does not attempt a refutation of materialism in this essay, noting only that if mind could be completely reduced to matter morality would not be possible: "moral consciousness can exist only to the extent that there is disagreement between nature and morality" (EA 10). Many philosophers have argued that materialism denies free will, which makes ethics impossible. But Beauvoir seems to be pursuing a different line of reasoning here, that is, that the relative independence of consciousness, its ability to transcend material conditions, is shown by the very experience of moral obligation. Humans judge that the way things are is not the way they ought to be and set about to change them.[6]

The ambiguity of human existence not only makes ethics possible. The dependence of consciousness on the body, which is at the mercy of external forces, the dependence of my life on the lives of others, is the feature of human life that makes ethics necessary. If each human consciousness really were "a sovereign and unique subject" (EA 7) over which the forces of nature and the wills of others had no power, there would be no need for morality. Because it is ambiguous, human existence is fragile. Since human beings can be abandoned, hurt, and killed, morality is a central concern of human life. Furthermore, the dependence of consciousness on the body is what renders humans ultimately vulnerable to moral judgment. As Beauvoir argues in her discussion of violence, sometimes the only way to reach those who have hurt, who have killed, is through their bodies.

Thus it is humans' hybrid nature—their ambiguous existence—that makes ethics both possible and necessary. Beauvoir goes on to assert that existentialism is the only philosophy that faces up to the basic ambiguity of human life.⁷ (At least Beauvoir's existentialism does. Sartre makes use of a slightly different ontological framework, as I will soon discuss.) Thus for Beauvoir not only is existentialism able to provide the foundation for an ethics, which many critics have denied, it is better positioned to do so than are other philosophies. This is because an existentialist ethics is, as Beauvoir's title proclaims, an ethics of ambiguity. Only an ethics of ambiguity can do justice to "the truth of life and death, of my solitude and my bond with the world, of my freedom and my servitude, of the insignificance and the sovereign importance of each man and all men" (EA 9).

Beauvoir's Use of Sartre's Ontology

How exactly does existentialism provide the philosophical basis for Beauvoir's ethics of ambiguity? Beauvoir's thesis is that human freedom is the source of moral obligation. Because we are free, she argues, we should completely realize our freedom by accepting its burdens rather than running from them. However—and this is the surprising new angle that Beauvoir brings to existentialist thought—my realizing my freedom does not necessarily conflict with others realizing their freedom. Not only does others' freedom not limit my own freedom, in order for me to completely realize my own freedom I require the freedom of others and thus have a moral obligation to defend and nurture this freedom. The starting point for this argument is a statement that she says comes from *Being and Nothingness:* "Man, Sartre tells us, is 'a being who *makes himself* a lack of being *in order that there might be* being'" (EA 11). Beauvoir uses this statement to encapsulate some basic precepts of existentialist ontology.

To explain what Beauvoir means to convey by this statement requires a brief overview of the ontology Sartre lays out in *Being and*

Nothingness. Beauvoir asserts that existentialism is a philosophy of ambiguity. However, Sartre's ontology is a dualistic one in which what exists is divided up into "two regions without communication" (BN lxiii): the for-itself—consciousness—and the in-itself—non-conscious reality. Thus, to return to the quote Beauvoir uses, the being that the for-itself lacks is the in-itself. Furthermore, the for-itself makes itself a lack of being by nihilating the in-itself. To demonstrate this thesis Sartre gives the example of searching for Pierre in the café. The busy café is full until he enters looking for someone who is not there. Thus, "Man is the being through whom nothingness comes to the world" (BN 24). Consciousness or the for-itself is a lack of being and this lack of being springs from its own activities.

The second part of this statement she quotes is more crucial for Beauvoir's project of founding an existentialist ethics. It claims that humans make themselves a lack of being in order that there might be being. Sartre makes a similar claim in *Being and Nothingness*: "the for-itself is . . . the nothingness whereby 'there is' being" (BN 181).[8] This last statement of Sartre's has a deliberately paradoxical ring to it, but it is easily understandable as a reinterpretation of Husserl's thesis about the intentionality of consciousness. Husserl's original insight is that all consciousness is consciousness *of* something. What consciousness is conscious of is something meaningful. Sartre ties the production of this meaning back to consciousness, as does Husserl.[9] In Husserl's terms, consciousness constitutes the meaning of objects in the world, and the meaning of the world itself. For, as Sartre says, the in-itself is not capable on its own of achieving the unity of a world. Consciousness, which is a lack of being, brings about that there is a world, or being. For this reason Beauvoir says that existentialism holds that a human is "a being who makes himself a lack of being in order that there might be being."

Yet Sartre departs radically from Husserl in retaining the category of the in-itself, a category of being existing apart from and underlying the for-itself. Husserl refrains from all questions about whether the objects we are conscious of actually exist. For him there is no category of being existing separate from consciousness. Furthermore, while the meaning of being originates through consciousness for Sartre, this "adds nothing" to being: "the fact of revealing being as totality does not touch being any more than the fact of counting two cups on the table touches the existence or nature of either of them" (BN 181).

Strictly speaking, then, the being that exists because humans exist as a lack of being is not being *per se* or the in-itself according to Sartre's ontology. It is the being that appears to consciousness or what Sartre calls the "phenomenon of being," to distinguish it from the being of phenomena or the realm of "non-conscious and transphenomenal being" (BN lxii) that Sartre claims to prove in his "ontological proof" is implied by the revealing activities of consciousness itself. But, as the quotes I have taken from *Being and Nothingness* demonstrate, Sartre himself does not stick to this more exact terminology, often speaking of being when he means the phenomenon of being and sometimes equating being with the world. Beauvoir also uses the term being in this loose sense in *The Ethics of Ambiguity*, and equates being with the world, that is, the world revealed to human consciousness.

Beauvoir builds on this ontological framework set up in *Being and Nothingness* in the beginning stages of her argument. Furthermore, her central thesis about the basic ambiguity of human existence presupposes an opposition between two categories of being similar to the for-itself and in-itself. According to her there is matter and there is consciousness and the human being is some strange blending of both. However, Beauvoir's ontology differs slightly from Sartre's. Beauvoir stresses the dark, submerged links between the nonconscious and the conscious more than he does. Sartre says that the in-itself and the for-itself are regions without communication, whereas for her: "Man is still part of the world of which he is a consciousness." In this regard Beauvoir's orientation appears closer to that of Merleau-Ponty than to Sartre. Elsewhere Beauvoir says that for Merleau-Ponty consciousness "is not a pure for-itself, or to use Hegel's phrase which Sartre has taken up, a 'hole in being'; but rather 'a hollow, a fold', which has been made and which can be unmade."[10] Although she does not use these same words, this description could almost be used to characterize her own position.

Secondly, in Beauvoir's description of this relation it is material reality which is seen to impinge on consciousness, rather than consciousness impinging on or negating the in-itself as in Sartre's ontology. A human, she says, "experiences himself as a thing crushed by the dark weight of other things." She observes that one of the central ironies of technological progress is that it has led to weapons that can turn the powers of nature against us to an extent undreamt of previously. Death is the irrefutable proof that consciousness exists at the mercy of external forces.

On the other hand, Sartre's language when he talks of the for-itself nihilating the in-itself suggests that humans' basic relation to nonconscious reality is one of domination. Consciousness is envisioned as a devouring consciousness, reminiscent of the life-devouring form of desire described at one point in Hegel's *Phenomenology of Spirit*.[11] Perhaps the dominating stance that one consciousness takes towards another consciousness in Sartre's analysis of being-for-others is prefigured in the nihilating stance that consciousness takes towards the in-itself in his ontology. The ironic thing is that for Sartre, although the for-itself exists as the constant nihilation of the in-itself, this nihilation never actually achieves any hold on the in-itself, for these two regions are regions without communication. In this regard Sartre's ontology differs radically from the more naturalistic ontologies of Marx and Aristotle, to which human interaction with nonorganic nature is central. This failure of the for-itself to actually "touch being" is perhaps one reason why humans are a "useless passion" for Sartre.

By contrast, one concrete example that Beauvoir gives of making oneself a lack of being in order that there be being presupposes that there is a basic urge to merge with nature rather than to dominate it. A human makes himself a lack of being by "uprooting himself from the world," she says, which goes against a deep desire: "I should like to be the landscape which I am contemplating, I should like this sky, this quiet water to think themselves within me, that it might be I whom they express in flesh and bone" (EA 12). Beauvoir refers to this desire to become one with nature in other works, as does Albert Camus in one of his essays.[12] In *The Second Sex* she gives a psychological explanation of its origins, tracing it back to the anguish caused when the infant is "separated more or less brutally from the nourishing body" of the mother at around six months of age:

> Man experiences this desertion with anguish. Fleeing his freedom, his subjectivity, he would fain lose himself in the bosom of the Whole. This is the origin of his cosmic and pantheistic dreams, of his longing for oblivion, for sleep, for ecstasy, for death. He never succeeds in abolishing his separate ego, but he wants at least to attain the solidity of the in-itself, to be petrified into a thing. (DS II 14; TSS 268–69)[13]

In *The Ethics of Ambiguity* Beauvoir emphasizes that humans' failure to realize this basic desire is not a loss but rather a gain. For by making ourselves a lack of being we remain at a distance from nature. Due to this distance the sky and the water exist before us.[14]

For Beauvoir, then, the realm of nonconscious being has more power over conscious beings than it does for Sartre. Her thesis about human ambiguity makes use of an opposition between two poles of human existence that correspond roughly to Sartre's concepts of the for-itself and the in-itself. Sartre stresses how the for-itself constantly negates the in-itself or material reality. Beauvoir stresses instead that we cannot escape our existence as material beings and suggests that we sometimes even yearn to succumb to it. Although she uses a quote she says comes from *Being and Nothingness* as the starting point of her argument, she gives a noticeably different twist to her existentialist ontology. Furthermore, the idea that the existence of the world is tied to human consciousness is not exactly a new one for her. As I showed in the last chapter, it is woven into several of her previous novels.

Ontological Freedom vs. Moral Freedom

Beauvoir declares in "L'Existentialisme et la sagesse des nations" that existentialism equates subjectivity with freedom. In his ontological scheme Sartre also equates the for-itself with freedom: "this possibility which human reality has to secrete a nothingness which isolates it—it is *freedom*" (BN 24). Beauvoir assumes the existence of human freedom as her starting point. It is also the ideal of her ethics. Her ethics is an existentialist ethics above all because it is an ethics of freedom.

It is impossible, however, to base an ethics on freedom if freedom is equated solely with subjectivity. The consequence of this identification is that, as Beauvoir says, "Every man is originally free" (EA 25). (Sartre puts it more dramatically in *Being and Nothingness*: we are condemned to be free.) But certainly not everyone acts morally. Thus for Beauvoir, to be moral involves not just being free, but willing oneself free. Yet, given our original freedom, this idea seems almost contradictory. Beauvoir realizes the problem here: "What meaning can there be in the words to *will oneself* free, since at the beginning we *are* free" (EA 24).

The only way out of this impasse for Beauvoir is to posit two different levels of freedom. Indeed, in order to provide a foundation for existentialist ethics she must make such a move. Beauvoir calls these two types of freedom "natural freedom" and "moral freedom."[15] Instead of using the phrase "natural freedom," which is potentially misleading, I will refer to this first type of freedom as "ontological freedom."[16] (There is no freedom in nature, after all, and no such thing as human nature for existentialism.) It is this type of freedom that Sartre is concerned with in *Being and Nothingness*: this is the freedom revealed in anguish and fled from in bad faith.

For Beauvoir, though, there is another level of freedom that pertains specifically to morality. This other level of freedom, moral freedom, is possible because there are two different ways that one can respond to the fact of one's ontological freedom. Although one cannot will oneself *not* to be free, because freedom is an ontological structure of human existence, one can fail to choose to will oneself free. Since one is always free, one can, and indeed one must, freely choose what attitude to take to one's own freedom. One can persist in the vain desire to be and not will oneself free. Or one can will oneself free by accepting one's freedom and actively making oneself a lack of being. If a person chooses the latter option then he or she achieves moral freedom.

Although Sartre does not set up two different levels of freedom as Beauvoir does, what he says in *Being and Nothingness* assumes that there is this reflexive aspect to freedom as well. Only because freedom can stand in relation to itself is bad faith, as Sartre calls it, possible. Bad faith is an attitude that we choose to take to the fact of our basic freedom: we choose to flee it. What Beauvoir describes as choosing not to will oneself free has obvious parallels to what Sartre describes as bad faith. But Beauvoir, I will show next, goes into much greater detail than Sartre does about the various different ways that one can fail to fully assume one's freedom and her account departs in some important ways from his.

Ways to Fail to Realize Moral Freedom

In the second section of *The Ethics of Ambiguity*, "Personal Freedom and Others," Beauvoir designates a series of personality types, each of which represents a different way people can fail to will themselves free. As this failure admits of degrees, each represents a progressively higher stage in the development of moral freedom. These five figures are, starting from the bottom rung of the ladder, the sub-man, the serious man, the nihilist, the adventurer, and the passionate man. Beauvoir gives a few concrete examples of people who fit in these categories. In the same spirit I offer a few more.

The first failure to come to grips with human freedom that Beauvoir explores is what she calls "the sub-man." (Some critics have complained that Sartre always singles out women to serve as examples of bad faith.[17] By contrast Beauvoir's examples of ethical failure are all male, which might not mean much, because Beauvoir, writing before the days of sex-neutral usage, usually uses the term "man" to stand for all humans.) The sub-man expresses a "fundamental fear in the face of existence" (EA 42), that is, his existence as a lack of being, through a continuous rejection of this existence and the world that is disclosed by it. He lacks affect: "He discovers around him only an insignificant and dull world. How could this naked world arouse within him any desire to feel, to understand, to live?" (EA 43). Constantly bewildered by the events in which he is continually swept up, he tries to elude not only awareness of what is going on around him, but his awareness of himself as a consciousness as well. Yet he can never succeed in reducing his presence to the world to the presence of an object in the world. As Beauvoir stresses in her discussion of ambiguity, a human is a material being, but never wholly a material being.

It is illuminating to compare Beauvoir's sub-man to the character of Meursault in Camus's *The Stranger* published in 1942. Beauvoir does not mention this work in her discussion of the sub-man in *The Ethics of Ambiguity*, but she does mention it in *Pyrrhus et Cinéas*, where she describes an attitude of detachment from the world similar to that assumed by the sub-man (see PC 14-15). Camus's character's strange passivity and flat truncated perceptions fit Beauvoir's description of the sub-man well, as does his lack of moral scruples. This lack of scruples is demonstrated in his connivance with the dubious character of Raymond, who beats up his lover and her brother and embroils Meursault in the series of events leading up to Meursault's murder of the Arab.

Camus's character raises an interesting ethical question, which Beauvoir's analysis of the sub-man can help answer: What guilt does

Meursault bear for his actions? Not intending to do anything, he did not intend to do wrong. But if Meursault did not intend to do what he did, how can he be condemned for it? Deontological ethics, at least, locates the moral worth of an action in the agent's intention. According to existentialist ethics, the guilt of a figure like Meursault is tied not to what his intentions were, but rather to his original choice not to assume the challenge of existing as a free human being. The sub-man fails—rather miserably—to achieve moral freedom because he tries to blank out the way that his ontological freedom constantly implicates him in events and the lives of others. But he cannot; he remains responsible for his existence, although he attempts to avoid taking any responsibility for his actions.

The moral failings of the sub-man can be illuminated even better in another example. Beauvoir reminds us that: "the sub-man is not a harmless creature. . . . In lynchings, in pograms, in all the great bloody movements organized by the fanaticism of seriousness and passion, . . . those who do the actual dirty work are recruited from among the sub-men" (EA 44). The Nazi functionary Adolf Eichmann whose 1961 trial Hannah Arendt wrote about in her *Eichmann in Jerusalem* certainly fits this description. Or to be more accurate, he should be located on that threshold where the sub-man passes over into the serious man in Beauvoir's scheme. Unable to annihilate his own subjectivity, the sub-man clutches in terror at certain social values that he then puts beyond question. Eichmann himself insisted that he lived his life according to Kantian moral precepts, but as Arendt points out, this claim is ridiculous. Eichmann changed Kant's injunction to always act according to the moral law into the command to always follow the law, period. Arendt's description of how the young Eichmann drifted from one school and career failure to the next ("I don't know, everything was as if I was under a spell")[18] certainly brings Beauvoir's sub-man to mind. And Eichmann's own account of what he got from his involvement with the Nazis fits her account of why the sub-man turns to serious values. Eichmann says that Germany's official defeat on May 8, 1945 overwhelmed him because:

> I sensed I would have to live a leaderless and difficult individual life, I would receive no directives from anybody, no orders and commands would any longer be issued to me, no pertinent ordinances would be there to consult—in brief, a life never known to me before lay before me.[19]

In light of Beauvoir's argument, which I will soon unfold, that moral freedom involves acknowledging the freedom of others, it is significant that one of Eichmann's greatest failings was his complete inability "to think from the standpoint of someone else."[20] This alone would have kept him from adopting the standpoint of Kantian morality.

Once the transition from the sub-man to the serious man is truly complete, the individual finds itself on a little more stable ground. The attitude taken by the serious man that certain values are eternal and immutable is the most widespread human attitude, Beauvoir asserts. She implies that many ethical systems, even those which appeal not to religious sanction but, like the liberal political tradition, to some underlying conception of human nature, serve simply as a way for humans to shield themselves from the full consequences of their ontological freedom. She recognizes that she is not the first to point out the error and folly of the serious man. Hegel, Kierkegaard, and Nietzsche also do so—and Sartre, of course: "*Being and Nothingness* is in large part a description of the serious man and his universe" (EA 46). For here bad faith reigns supreme. The serious man masks his own creation of values the way that a deluded woman who writes herself love letters pretends they were sent by someone else (see EA 47).

Interestingly enough, the sub-man cannot be accused of such subterfuge. (Camus's character Meursault is honest to a fault.) And for Beauvoir the sub-man represents an even greater capitulation of freedom than the serious man does. The implication is that bad faith is not the only, or even the worst, moral failing in her ethics.

Like the sub-man, the serious man's relations to others is flawed by a deep insensitivity. The serious man is dangerous, Beauvoir says, because he will so readily sacrifice others for the values he unquestioningly accepts. Beauvoir gives the example of the colonialist bulldozing a highway through the jungle, leaving human misery in its wake. But she also notes that for the revolutionary the revolution can become an inhuman idol. This is the error that the political realists on the Left she discusses in "Idéalisme moral et réalisme politique" fall prey to.

The next personality type that Beauvoir depicts, the nihilist, can be even more murderous than the serious man. Beauvoir sees this attitude arising when the serious man gives up his attempt to endow the human world of values with the status of being. The sudden deflation of values that have been heretofore unquestioned leads to a terrible crisis. Since there is nothing stable external to him to anchor meanings the nihilist concludes that there is no meaning and a void opens at his feet. This response to the collapse of serious values is the same one described by Nietzsche in his parable about the death of God in *The Gay Science*. In Beauvoir's account, however, the nihilist, surrounded by a world that to him is devoid of meaning, is driven to make himself nothing as well. Beauvoir is aware of the possibilities for confusion here. For Sartre himself says that man is the being by whom nothingness enters the world, a being who is not what he is and is what he is not. But the nihilist does not want to live his nothingness in this way. Rather, as Beauvoir says: "he conceives his annihilation in a substantial way." Instead of making himself a lack of being, the lack of being that he in fact is, the nihilist is still stuck at the level of wanting to be, but what it is that he wants to be is nothing, that is, nothing as "another sort of being" (EA 52).

Of course, the one way literally to annihilate oneself in a substantial way is suicide. But the nihilist's drive to make himself nothing can also be realized through the destruction of other human beings. This is because the existence of other human beings reflects back to him his own existence. Others disclose him as a presence to the world, that is, as another subject, which frustrates his desire to be nothing even more. Thus nihilism often merges the "will for suicide" with a will to power, as for example, when people under the sway of such ideologies as Nazism literally make themselves into the means by which "nothingness comes into the world" (EA 56).

Nihilism does not have to have quite such dire consequences. It also can be played out at a cultural level. Some artists (she mentions Sartre's portrait of Baudelaire in this regard) maintain serious values just "in order to trample on them" (EA 53). In the incoherence achieved by Dadaism, on the other hand, she sees the almost perfect realization of the nihilist project: "The constant negation of the word by the word, the act by the act, of art by art" (EA 54). But the actual life histories of various surrealists show that this attitude is not stable and can diverge to take different forms: suicide, physical dissipation, "moral suicide," reform. The irony is that even those surrealists who remained faithful to their original project could not help slipping into the stance of seriousness: "The negation of aesthetic, spiritual, and moral values has become an ethics" (EA 55). Perhaps the ultimate irony is that some have even managed to create serious works of art. The extent to which the nihilistic stance of surrealism is still a feature of the contemporary art scene today would be an interesting subject of debate.

As I said, there is a hierarchy implicit in the order in which Beauvoir presents the series of personality types in this section of *The Ethics of Ambiguity*. The sub-man, whom she discusses first, inspires universal contempt, even more so than the serious man, who, Beauvoir acknowledges, has been under concerted intellectual attack for close to one hundred years at this point. The nihilist, however, at least has reached the stage in the realization of his ontological freedom where he *can* serve as an ally of a person who seeks genuine freedom. Together they can "contest the serious world" (EA 57). But Beauvoir also points out that systematic nihilism can result in tyranny and destruction, which the genuinely free person in his or her commitment to the freedom of others must combat.

The adventurer, the next figure she explores, takes a stance that is "very close to a genuinely moral attitude" (EA 59). Beauvoir herself was something of an adventurer. In her memoirs she records her passion for taking cross-country hikes into uncharted terrain, sometimes alone, sometimes impatiently dragging along less vigorous companions. Her treatment of the character of the explorer Carlier in *All Men Are Mortal* also shows her fascination with such figures. The adventurer is to be admired according to her because, unlike the nihilist, he embraces his existence as lack of being; he gives up wanting to be. Furthermore, he knows that there is no external justification for his existence, but this does not set him off in a fury of destruction. He does not look to eternal values, or even socially constituted ones, to condone his exploits. He acts just for the sake of acting, for the sake of expending his constantly renewed energy, of expressing his vitality and the joy he takes in life.

The emphasis that Beauvoir places on the joy with which the adventurer faces his unjustified existence is significant. One criticism of existentialism that Beauvoir could not stomach was that it was a philosophy of gloom and doom. In *The Ethics of Ambiguity* and elsewhere Beauvoir insists that an authentic existence is one that is open to great joy. In her memoirs she emphasized that this was a central feature of her own experience of life.

What then keeps the adventurer from achieving the genuinely authentic attitude of moral freedom? First, Beauvoir notes, sometimes this stance can hide quite different agendas. A person with no other serious commitments can still pursue the serious values of fame and fortune. However, the real moral failure of the adventurer lies in his relations with other people. His downfall inevitably results from the same truth that Blomart discovers in *The Blood of Others*: "Every undertaking unfolds in a human world and affects men" (EA 60). Although the adventurous man tries to hold himself at a distance from others and their values, he cannot. He ends up manipulating them to further his projects. His basic moral failing is regarding "mankind as indifferent matter destined to support the game of his existence" (EA 62).

The adventurers that we know the most about are those who succumb to another temptation, a temptation that arises out of their own lucidity about their predicament. They understand that the only meaning that their lives have is the one that they themselves give it, for they are not engaged in a shared enterprise with others. When they die, the meaning of their lives dies too. So it is up to them alone to immortalize themselves, which they do by writing books or by encouraging a cult of personality to form around them: "For want of a work, many desire to bequeath their own personality to posterity: at least during their lifetime they need the approval of a few faithful" (EA 63). Ironically, this desire betrays a need for others as a means to affirm one's own existence, just that aspect of life that they have ignored or rejected.

But the one person Beauvoir mentions who did write about his exploits transcended the stance of the adventurer according to her: T. E. Lawrence. Lawrence was a genuinely free man, because he "was so concerned about the lives of his companions and the freedom of others, so tormented by the human problems which all action raises" (EA 61).[21] A better example might be the Danish writer Isak Dinesen, who wrote memoirs of her adventures in Africa. Although Dinesen defied conventional expectations and led a life of great freedom for a European woman of her era, she was not too concerned with the freedom of others. The fact that it was the institution of colonialism that made such a life possible never seemed even to occur to her. She also assiduously cultivated an image of herself.

The adventurer is not motivated in his quest by the values that the rest of the world takes seriously, but then he is not really motivated by any end at all. He is, Beauvoir remarks, detached from his goal. In this respect he is the antithesis of the next personality type that Beauvoir discusses, the passionate man. The passionate man is tremendously attached to the object of his passion. It is all-important to him. But, unlike the serious man, the passionate man realizes that the importance of this object depends entirely on his passion. The serious man subscribes to certain eternal ideals, for example, truth and beauty. The passionate man loves only this particular person or object, in spite of, or even because of, its imperfections. In this way the attitude of the passionate man represents an advance over that of the serious man. As Beauvoir says, "real passion asserts the subjectivity of its involvement" (EA 64). In his desire the passionate man experiences his lack of being. Furthermore, his desire serves to add an additional level of meaning to the human world. Thus it is a disclosure of being in Beauvoir's sense.

Beauvoir makes a distinction between generous and maniacal passions, however. In maniacal passion the passionate man seeks to possess the object of passion and by means of it to finally attain to the level of being. It is as though the passionate man is convinced that through the strength of his desire alone he can bestow being on the object of his desire, and then by possessing this object bestow being on himself. He is not in bad faith like the serious man. Unlike the deluded woman who pretends that the letter she holds in her hands was written by her lover not herself, the passionate man acknowledges he has written the letter but hopes to overcome this defect by the sheer strength of his desire to believe that the words are true. He is not deceiving himself about the source of the value of his beloved, though he is deceiving himself that he can possess her or it.

The maniacally passionate man falls short of moral freedom, also, in that he encloses himself in solitude. No one else can possibly grasp the full value of this being he cherishes so much; true communication with him is impossible. Other people lose all value when compared with the object of his passion. If, acting on this conviction, he uses others as means to pursue his passion, then he lapses into what Beauvoir calls a partial nihilism. Beauvoir does not discuss how passion can become even more nihilistic when the passionate man, furious because he cannot possess the object of his love, comes to destroy it. If this object is, as it often is, another person, passion can have the same fatal consequences for others that nihilism does.

Indeed it is a notable feature of Beauvoir's description of the passionate man, and not necessarily a failing of it, that it remains ambiguous whether the object of his passion is another person or not. It can be in the case of "amorous passion," but it also can be just a "rare treasure" (EA 64–65). The implication is that it is almost the same in either case. When the target of the passionate man's ardor is another person then that person becomes like an object in some sense. Of course, the beloved is not in this way stripped of her subjectivity in the way the war crimes victims Beauvoir describes in "Oeil pour oeil" are. The object of passion, even when it *is* a material object, is not a mere thing. But insofar as the passionate man hopes to possess the object of his passion it cannot be recognized as a free subject by him. Only if the passionate man accepts the distance that necessarily separates him from his beloved instead of trying to eliminate that distance, can he acknowledge the loved one as another free subject, Beauvoir argues. In this way passion can be converted to moral freedom. One cannot love a material object in this way: "One cannot love a pure thing in its independence and its separation, for the thing does not have positive independence" (EA 67). But one can devote oneself to something material in the cause of freedom insofar as it, say a homeland or an artwork, opens up possibilities to other human freedoms.

Beauvoir includes a chapter in *The Second Sex* entitled "The Woman in Love." Can what Beauvoir says about the passionate man in *The Ethics of Ambiguity* serve as a complementary description of the man in love? There are interesting similarities and differences between the two accounts. In *The Second Sex* Beauvoir contends that men can never attain the level of grand passion, because "they never abdicate completely" (DS II 477; TSS 642); they always want to possess the object of their passion. This is just the failing ascribed to the passionate man in *The Ethics of Ambiguity*. Women's passion, on the other hand, is shown to lead to a complete abdication, and to various exquisitely refined forms of misery. Significantly, the same Mlle. de Lespinasse, whose love letters are used in *The Ethics of Ambiguity* to describe how genuine love accepts the wrench that the beloved's separation from her involves, appears in *The Second Sex* in quite a different guise. Here Mlle. de Lespinasse complains bitterly: "Ah, God! If you only knew how my days are, what my life is like deprived of the interest and pleasure of seeing you!" (DS II 492; TSS 656). Perhaps by the time she came to write *The Second Sex* Beauvoir had decided that the ideal of genuine love is realized more rarely than she once thought. Certainly by this time she has begun to put more emphasis on the conditions under which love relationships are formed and on the social conditions of freedom generally.

Beauvoir's Concept of Disclosure

In my overview of Beauvoir's analysis of these five character types I have indicated how according to her each of them fails to accept others as genuinely free subjects. At the end of her presentation of them Beauvoir concludes: "Thus we can see that no existence can be validly fulfilled if it is limited to itself. It appeals to the existence of others" (EA 67). But in that part of Beauvoir's argument that I have recounted so far she has only asserted that in order to achieve moral freedom one must genuinely accept one's existence as a lack of being. In my treatment of the sub-man, nihilist, and serious man I have shown how each of them fails to live up to this challenge. But now I must show how the failure of each of these five character types to fully assume their own freedom is connected with their refusal to fully acknowledge others as free. Or, to put it conversely, I must unfold Beauvoir's argument as to why moral freedom necessarily entails a recognition of and commitment to others' freedom.

This argument is the centerpiece of *The Ethics of Ambiguity.* In my presentation of it I will concentrate on two separate claims she makes that will turn out to be closely interrelated. They are that (1) "the existence of others as a freedom defines my situation and is even the condition of my own freedom" (EA 91) and (2) "To will oneself free is also to will others free" (EA 73).

The first part of the first claim, that "the existence of others as a freedom defines my situation," is really a restatement of the thesis that Beauvoir argues for in *Pyrrhus et Cinéas.* There she argues that others' actions serve as the point of departure for all of my actions and that only the existence of others guarantees that my actions have significance. My freedom would have no meaning unless it unfolded against a backdrop of something given for it. In *The Ethics of Ambiguity,* however, she claims that the existence of others has even a greater relevance for my freedom than just to serve as a backdrop to my actions in this way. Here she says that the existence of other freedoms is *even* the condition of my own freedom. In philosophical terms to say that something is the condition of something else is to say that the second thing would not exist unless the first thing did. But how could it be that my freedom depends on the existence of other freedoms?

In order to explain how the existence of other freedoms is the condition of my own freedom I must turn once again to the thesis that Beauvoir uses as a beginning point in *The Ethics of Ambiguity*: humans make themselves a lack of being in order that there might be being. I have explained at some length what making oneself a lack of being means for Beauvoir. Now I need to return to the subject of how existing as a lack of being, or as a free conscious agent, makes it possible that there is being. As I noted earlier, for Beauvoir being here means what Sartre calls the phenomenon of being, or the realm of being that is present to human consciousness. In Beauvoir's conception, then, being is equivalent to "the human world in which each object is penetrated with human meanings" (EA 74). These meanings can be traced back, à la Husserl, to the meaning-producing activities of consciousness, and more generally for Beauvoir back to human praxis as a whole. Thus it is only because human beings are a lack of being, that is, conscious freely acting agents, that the human world or being exists.

Beauvoir uses another locution when describing the basic relation between human subjectivity and the human world. She says that it is by means of human freedom that being is disclosed: "It is not in vain that man nullifies being. Thanks to him, being is disclosed" (EA 12). This locution is preferable perhaps because, unlike all this talk of making being be, it avoids leaving any impression that Beauvoir subscribes to some form of subjective idealism. Being is not so much, as it were, manufactured by human freedom as disclosed as meaningful by it.

The term "disclose" has an undeniably Heideggerian ring to it, which is partly due to the translation. Beauvoir uses the French word *dévoiler* in these passages, which can also be translated into English as "unveil." This is rendered by her translator as "disclose," which is also the accepted English translation of Heidegger's term *erschliessen*.[22] But this coincidence is telling, for Beauvoir undoubtedly was influenced by Heidegger's concept of Being-in-the-world in constructing the model of human-world relations she uses in *The Ethics of Ambiguity*. Nonetheless, for her *dévoilement* does not mean exactly what *Erschlossenheit* does for Heidegger. Not surprisingly, Beauvoir stresses the active nature of humans' disclosure of the world more than Heidegger does. For Heidegger what is "there" has always already somehow been disclosed.[23]

But what sort of freedom is it that is involved in the disclosure of being? For Beauvoir distinguishes between two types of freedom in this work. It turns out that both ontological freedom and moral freedom disclose the world, but that a different attitude is taken towards this disclosure in each. Beauvoir says that humans cannot help disclosing being in some way or another: "men are always disclosing being, in Buchenwald as well as in the blue isles of the Pacific, in hovels as well as in palaces" (EA 74). Even the sub-man in Beauvoir's depiction of him could not manage to reduce himself to an inanimate object: he remained a presence to the world. Thus even at the level of ontological freedom, which is shared by all, human existence involves a disclosure of a world, however impoverished that world might be.

Furthermore, even at this level the realm of being that is disclosed through freedom is the human world "penetrated with human meanings" (EA 74), because there is no other world to disclose. The human world depends on the existence of other human beings. The meanings with which it is saturated do not originate in me alone. They are intersubjectively constituted, to use the phrase Husserl uses in his last work, the *Crisis*. The existence of other subjects is the condition of the existence of the human world. Thus if human freedom, even at the level of bare ontological freedom, is always at the same time a disclosure of a world, then the existence of other human subjects is the condition of this freedom. As Beauvoir puts it more succinctly: "One can reveal the world only on a basis revealed by other men" (EA 71).

For this reason none of the figures that Beauvoir depicts in the second section of *The Ethics of Ambiguity* can deny the significance of other people within the world, try as they might. Others continually give meaning to the world that they jointly inhabit. Of these figures it is the nihilist who has the strongest reaction to the role others play in constituting the meaning of the world. The presence of others presents a major stumbling block for the nihilist's desire to be nothing, because others disclose him as a member of this human world. This is the reason why others must be obliterated: "If he [the nihilist] wills himself to be nothing, all mankind must also be annihilated, otherwise by means of the presence of this world that the other reveals he meets himself as a presence in the world" (EA 55).

In this same vein Beauvoir critiques the nihilistic stance Spirit assumes at the beginning of Hegel's Master/Slave Dialectic, where "each consciousness seeks the death of the other." To actually follow this motto would be self-defeating: "If I really were everything there could be nothing beside me; the world would be empty. There would be nothing to possess, and I myself would be nothing" (EA 71). As I discussed before, this phrase from Hegel served as the epigraph of her first published novel, *She Came to Stay*, fittingly so, given the picture of interpersonal relations presented there. Her remarks on it in *The Ethics of Ambiguity* show the extent to which her view on the relations between subjects has changed.

So, even at the level of ontological freedom, freedom always disclos-es a world, and that world testifies to the presence of other freedoms. But a person should not be content to remain at the level of mere ontologi-cal freedom, Beauvoir holds. The challenge is to achieve an authentic realization of one's ontological freedom—to rise to the level of moral freedom. The next question becomes: what relation to the world is involved in moral freedom? How is the world disclosed through it?

The key is whether one desires or wills the disclosure of being. If one does, then one is on the road to achieving moral freedom: "To wish for the disclosure of the world and to assert oneself as a freedom are one and the same movement" (EA 24). Beauvoir's figures of the sub-man and the nihilist provide examples of people who do not desire the disclosure of the world. The nihilist attempts to stop this process, while the sub-man refuses to participate in it. Or instead of willing to disclose being, one can get caught up in the alternative desire to achieve the status of being oneself. All humans are haunted by this desire, both Beauvoir and Sartre assert, because down deep they grasp their lack of being.

This desire for being takes different forms and can be manifested in a wide variety of human behaviors. To Sartre the desire for being is ultimately the desire to achieve the synthesis of the for-itself and the in-itself that is God. Beauvoir suggests instead that humans possess a desire to slip back into the nature from which they emerged, "to be nothing but a white ripple rising and disappearing into the even sur-face of the water" (BO 186). In her novels Beauvoir depicts how the desire for being can give rise to inauthentic behavior. Hélène in *The*

Blood of Others looks to her love for Blomart to fill this need for being, a need that was filled earlier by her belief in God. Regina in *All Men Are Mortal* needs not just love, but the constant presence of an appreciative audience in order to feel that she exists. She even wants this audience, and thus her existence, to continue into perpetuity through Fosca's undying remembrance of her. But both these strategies fail, as do all human attempts to achieve being.

In *The Ethics of Ambiguity* Beauvoir tries to modify Sartre's grim pronouncement that man is a useless passion. It is true, she says, that humans are forever haunted by a desire that they can never satisfy: "It is not granted him to exist without tending toward this being which he will never be" (EA 13). But the desire to disclose being is another primary urge that humans have. And this is a desire that they can fulfill. Indeed as conscious beings they cannot help but disclose the world. The important thing is actively to will that disclosure. If they do then they can "coincide" with themselves, that is, with the lack of being that they are: "The original scheme of man is ambiguous: he wants to be and to the extent that he coincides with this wish, he fails. . . . But man also wills himself to be a disclosure of being, and if he coincides with this wish, he wins, for the fact is that the world becomes present by his presence in it" (EA 23). For Beauvoir, to be able to coincide with oneself in this way is a victory.

Willing Others Free

To a certain extent the connection between my freedom and the freedom of others holds true even at the level of ontological freedom, as I have explored. Yet it is at the level of moral freedom that the connection between my freedom and the freedom of others is the strongest. And it is this connection between my developing my own moral freedom and my working to further the moral freedom of others that Beauvoir is most concerned to draw out, for it is the source of my moral responsibilities to others. The morally free person is not only committed to preserving the ontological freedom of others by preserving their lives. Our ultimate responsibility, Beauvoir's ethics implies, is not the preservation of life, but the defense and nurturance of freedom. We are called on "to set freedom free"[24] by helping ontological freedom blossom into moral freedom.

But what exactly is the basis of this connection between my moral freedom and the moral freedom of others? This connection is most strongly expressed in the second claim that Beauvoir makes that I quoted previously: "To will oneself free is also to will others free." To will oneself free is equivalent to making oneself a lack of being by actively desiring to disclose the world. Whether humans want to be free or not they are ontologically free. And even if they do not desire to disclose being, they still do. But what they can and should do, Beauvoir asserts, is to actively assume this destiny. Only then is ontological freedom transformed into moral freedom.

But why in order for me to will myself free in this way must I also will others free? In order to bring out the connection here it is necessary to bring another factor into consideration. This factor is the role that the future plays in both my own existence and the existence of others. It makes no sense to speak of freedom except in relation to time. Sartre puts the relation between human temporality and freedom this way: "the condition on which human reality can deny all or part of the world is that human reality carry nothingness within itself as the nothing which separates its present from all its past" (BN 28). For Beauvoir this temporal dimension of human life is not so much a condition of freedom as inextricable from it: "without this particular movement which thrusts him toward the future man would not exist" (EA 118).

Beauvoir posits an underlying connection between an affirmation of human temporality and the development of moral freedom. The lack of temporal cohesion in children's experience keeps them from being full moral agents, she notes. In order to adopt a moral attitude towards one's actions one must be aware that what one does today will still matter tomorrow. This requires one to understand that in the future what is now the present will become the past. To act morally requires not only an ability to grasp the temporal continuity of human life, but also, for Beauvoir, the willingness to affirm it: "I can not genuinely desire an end today without desiring it through my whole existence, insofar as it is the future of this present moment and insofar as it is the surpassed past of days to come" (EA 27). An adult can fail to be morally free by trying to escape this temporal continuity by clinging to "the absurdity of the pure moment" (EA 26) as the sub-man attempts to do. A child's grasp of temporal dimension is restricted by other factors and this is one reason why children are not held to be morally responsible for their actions the way that adults are.

Of the three dimensions of the temporal continuum it is the future that is most central to my existence as a freedom: "The future is the definite direction of a particular transcendence and it is so closely bound up with the present that it composes with it a single temporal form" (EA 116). (Beauvoir mentions Heidegger's conception of temporality at this juncture in *The Ethics of Ambiguity*, but she also was influenced by Merleau-Ponty's treatment of temporality in his *Phenomenology of Perception*.[25]) Action can only unfold in the direction of the future. Therefore, the future is "the meaning and substance of all action" (EA 127). Human action, as distinct from random motion, is purposeful. The actions that I take now can look ahead to the next minute or the next century, but their significance necessarily transcends the present moment.

To say that only the future gives meaning to my present actions leads to a paradox, however, and the necessity for a resolution to this paradox motivates a key step in Beauvoir's argument. How can the future give meaning to my actions if it does not exist yet? There is no guarantee that any future state, no matter how fervently awaited, will come into existence. The indeterminacy of the future is entailed by the existence of human freedom. This is the reason why all deterministic theories of history find human freedom so problematic. In the third section of *The Ethics of Ambiguity* Beauvoir takes those systems of thought that claim to be able to see into the future severely to task. First there is Christianity, which, in predicting a Second Coming foretold by certain events but not causally linked to them, severs the future from the present and elevates it to the status of being, stripping it of its essence as temporal. Enlightenment thinkers reconnect the future to the present while at the same time envisaging it as something set and certain to come to pass: "Then, through the idea of progress, an idea of the future was elaborated in which its two aspects fused: the future appeared both as the meaning of our transcendence and as the immutability of being." This view is "hesitantly reflected in the systems of Hegel and Comte," (EA 116) and uncritically taken up by certain Marxists. Marx himself, Beauvoir notes, saw the emergence of the socialist state as only the beginning of real human history. But Marx was wrong to picture this final development as positive and harmonious: conflict is an essential feature of human history, she counters.[26] She endorses instead Trotsky's vision of the future as a permanent revolution.

Christians, Enlightenment proponents of progress, and the Marxists of her day are all wrong in their claims to be able to see into the future, because there *is* nothing there to see. The future does not exist yet; only insofar as it does not exist yet is it the future. They all make the mistake of conceiving of the future as a "Future-Thing" (EA 117), something that lies ahead of us on a path that we need only to walk down in order to make its absence in the present its presence in the future. This is the wrong way to understand temporality, because there is nothing now present in the future and there never will be.

It is because these systems of thought surreptitiously posit the future as something already existing that they are prone to resort to the moral posture that the end justifies the means. They forget that the end may never be attained, whereupon they will be left with only the means they have taken to bring it about, which will now have to be judged on their own merits. For Beauvoir a human being in choosing a particular end commits himself or herself to taking the means to realize it. But this end is created in choosing it; it does not already exist. It itself is in need of justification.

These reflections, however, only serve to deepen the paradox that I have sketched out: only the future can give meaning to my actions, but the future does not exist yet. Then how can it give meaning to my present actions? The way for Beauvoir to extricate herself from this paradox is to appeal to the existence of other free human agents. As Beauvoir puts it, others open the future for me: "As we have seen, my freedom, in order to fulfill itself, requires that it emerge into an open future: it is other men who open the future to me; it is they who, setting up the world of tomorrow, define my future" (EA 82). The meaning that is bestowed by the future on my actions comes from other free subjects who in concert with or in opposition to me create the future in the present through their projects and plans. Of course, this future too may never come to pass, but whether it does or not, it still serves to give meaning to my present actions.

When Beauvoir asserts that it is other humans who open up the future for me, the implication is that I cannot do this myself. I cannot create a future all by myself. Any idea of the future that I construct completely on my own must remain a fantasy. For example, I may decide that I have the solution to some contemporary political dilemma, but unless I engage myself with others this solution will never be realized. In order for my political views to be of any consequence, even to me, I must take the first steps toward political engagement, which necessarily involves me in other people's projects. Naturally, forces could prevent me from taking these steps. It is because we must rely on others to open the future for us, Beauvoir goes on to say, that oppression is possible—and hateful. Others can cut me off from a future by keeping me from freely interacting with other free agents.

So whereas *the* future does not exist, *a* future is always being sketched out in the plans and projects of interacting human beings and the meaning of my present action is drawn from this future. However, it is not the totality of others, the collective whole of humanity, that bestows meaning on my present actions. As Beauvoir points out: "Universal, absolute man exists nowhere" (EA 112). The general happiness promoted by utilitarian ethics is not the goal of actual living humans. She also argues against Hegel that separate finite human individuals cannot be encompassed within a rational whole. And she rejects the argument that the only alternative to the Hegelian view is that human history is unintelligible. Rather, human freedoms intertwine to the extent that they are engaged in concrete particular projects defined in terms of particular historical contexts. These different projects make up "a multiplicity of coherent ensembles" or "intelligible sequences" that can be comprehended "in the perspective of an ideal unity of the world" (EA 122).

Although the meaning this concrete group of individuals endows my actions with does not stretch indefinitely ahead into the future, it can survive my own death: "It is only by prolonging itself through the freedom of others that it [freedom] manages to surpass death itself and to realize itself as an indefinite unity" (EA 32). This projection of meaning into the future by a group of intertwined freedoms gives heroic deeds their significance and makes risking or sacrificing one's life more than just a foolhardy gesture. Thus when one takes it on oneself to make a sacrifice, one does not sacrifice oneself *for* others. Rather, strange as it may sound, one does it *with* others. Only if one is working with others in a joint project does one's sacrifice have meaning.

Through one's involvement in the historically rooted, distinct, concrete projects that I just mentioned one's own moral freedom is linked with that of others. One cannot attain moral freedom unless one is engaged with other humans who seek moral freedom as well— with others who seek to fulfill their existence as a lack of being by

throwing themselves into the future by means of their plans and projects thereby giving meaning to their acts and mine. Therefore, in
order to realize one's own moral freedom, one must insure somehow
that others can realize the full dimension of their existence as free
human beings. This is what Beauvoir means by her declaration that to
will oneself free is to will others free. Without this interaction with
others one plays out one's life in a mere charade of freedom.

For instance, a tyrant who actively suppresses the development of
others' freedom cuts himself off from such interaction and thus cannot realize moral freedom. For this reason Beauvoir feels justified in
making the rather bold assertion that "if the oppressor were aware
of the demands of his own freedom, he himself should have to
denounce oppression" (EA 96). Beauvoir supports this claim that
the oppressor himself should be interested in eliminating oppression
by paraphrasing Marx: "each one needs to have all men free" (EA
85). This message is also conveyed by the ending of Hegel's
Master/Slave Dialectic where the master is frustrated in his drive for
recognition and fails to achieve true self-consciousness. For
Beauvoir it is not so much that the tyrant cannot achieve recognition as that he is not truly free, which for her is a graver fate to suffer. It might seem contradictory to assert that a tyrant is not free, for
he can do most anything he wants. But the type of freedom that the
tyrant lacks is moral freedom, which is distinct from power or the
freedom to get what you want.

As I will argue in the next chapter, oppression robs people of the
opportunity to develop moral freedom. By depriving others of this
opportunity, the tyrant deprives himself of it too. The existence of
the moral freedom of others is the condition of one's own moral
freedom. To will oneself free is to actively desire to disclose the
world. To actively seek to disclose the world is to desire that others
exist who actively disclose it as well, to will "that there be men by
and for whom the world is endowed with human signification" (EA
71). The important point is that there be humans *by* whom the
world is endowed with human significations. The oppressor also
wants there to be other humans *for* whom the world is endowed
with human signification—the signification of his power. The
morally free person by contrast seeks the company of other active
free agents who also are shaping the world and the future. Moral
freedom is only attainable if others can realize the full dimension of

their existence in this way too. To make oneself a lack of being by actively disclosing the world requires furthering the freedom of others: "To want existence, to want to disclose the world, and to want men to be free are one and the same will" (EA 87).

Beauvoir's Ethics as an Existentialist Ethics

The original French title of *The Ethics of Ambiguity* is more equivocal than the title given the English translation. It is *Pour une morale de l'ambiguité*. This underlines the fact that Beauvoir did not intend to present a complete ethical system in this short work, if such a thing could even be possible within an existentialist framework. But even the French title indicates that Beauvoir was working towards developing an ethics congruent with the central tenets of existentialism. In this chapter I will analyze and assess the ethics that Beauvoir begins to lay out here. First I will compare Beauvoir's existentialist ethics to other approaches that have been taken to existentialist ethics. Then I will delineate the features of her ethics from a more general perspective and consider some possible objections against it.

Does Sartre Have an Ethics?

The obvious direction to turn when searching for another version of existentialist ethics is to Sartre. This goes against a common assumption, however, which is that there is really no distinction between Sartre's and Beauvoir's philosophical thought. Many commentators see Beauvoir simply to be applying Sartre's ideas in her novels and other works, at least in the period that predates *The Second Sex*. In the popular mind Sartre is usually identified as *the* existentialist and Beauvoir merely as his disciple. Beauvoir herself gave credence to this view by insisting in interviews later in life that it was Sartre who was the philosopher and not she and that *Being and Nothingness* was the sole philosophical influence on her work.[1] But this picture is coming increasingly under attack. One pair of writers even claims that Sartre took many of the central ideas of *Being and Nothingness* from a draft he read of Beauvoir's novel *She Came to Stay*.[2] Another scholar, Margaret A. Simons, has located Beauvoir's early diaries from the period before she met Sartre and claims that many of the central themes of existentialism are foreshadowed there.[3] Most Sartre scholars, unsurprisingly, reject these claims.[4]

Obviously this is a controversial issue. I will not take a position on it here, except to note that it deserves further research. Regardless of who originated the central ideas of existentialism, that Beauvoir was an existentialist is clear. She fully acknowledged it.[5] Although she never authored a systematic work on philosophy like *Being and Nothingness*, she published a number of philosophical essays. She had an advanced degree in philosophy and taught it for a number of years. Thus, her protestations to the contrary, she must be regarded as an existentialist philosopher in her own right.

Furthermore, her philosophical positions on a number of issues differ from Sartre's. In the last chapter I explored how her approach to certain topics deviates from Sartre's approach in *Being and Nothingness*. Most importantly for my purposes, her postulation in *The Ethics of Ambiguity* of another level of freedom, moral freedom, above and beyond the ontological freedom that all humans share, is a major departure from Sartre's conception of freedom. Even more strikingly, her thesis that I can achieve moral freedom only by working in tandem with other genuinely free agents is at odds with Sartre's analysis of self-other relations in *Being and Nothingness*. Beauvoir assumes that an intermingling of freedoms in pursuit of a joint goal is possible. Sartre, on the other hand, contends that "conflict is the original meaning of being-for-others" (BN 364). Even though Sartre acknowledges that humans do sometimes experience themselves joined in community with others, he says that this experience "could not constitute an onto-logical structure of human-reality" (BN 414). Solidarity with others is only experienced in the presence of what Sartre calls 'the Third', a consciousness set over against them. (In his later work, Sartre changes his views about human relationships. In his *Critique of Dialectical Reason* he even discusses how individuals can fuse together into a group. What I say about the differences between Beauvoir and Sartre here, and throughout this book, apply only to *Being and Nothingness*, not these later works.)

If Beauvoir was an existentialist philosopher in her own right and her philosophical positions differ from Sartre's in a number of key ways, then it makes sense to look to Sartre's work to compare their respective approaches to ethics. The problem with this strategy is that Sartre never produced an ethics. The collection of manuscripts published after his death as *Notebooks for an Ethics* show that he attempted to do so. But apparently he eventually gave up on the idea of writing an ethics because he came to the conclusion that the conditions humans live under would have to be radically changed by means of a socialist revolution for it to be possible even to talk seriously about an ethics.[6] (Additional lecture notes and manuscripts on ethics apparently exist from an even later period and their publication is eagerly awaited.[7])

Even though Sartre never published a philosophical work on ethics, it is still possible to turn to some of the other things he wrote to get some inkling of his thoughts on the subject. For instance, there are his literary writings. Beauvoir herself saw literature as a favored mode for expressing philosophical ideas. When one looks at some of the plays that Sartre wrote during the general period that Beauvoir wrote *The Ethics of Ambiguity* (for example, *The Flies*, 1943; *Morts sans sépulture*, 1946; *Dirty Hands*, 1948), one can make one generalization perhaps: Sartre is much more pessimistic about the possibility of moral action than she is. In them he questions whether it is ever possible to do the morally right thing. And even if it is, he implies, it is often pointless, because circumstances dictate that it never has the intended impact. In the end, however, the sheer volume of Sartre's literary production defeats any effort to discern a unified vision of humans' moral predicament and responsibilities in it.[8]

There remain three other places to look for Sartre's version of an existentialist ethics. There are the scattered remarks he makes in *Being and Nothingness* on the subject. Next there is the lecture he gave in 1945 subsequently published as a short essay called "Existentialism is a Humanism." And finally there are the posthumously published manuscripts I just referred to. I will say a little about each of these sources in turn.

Being and Nothingness

In the absence of a systematic work on ethics, many commentators have closely scrutinized the few remarks that Sartre makes on the subject in *Being and Nothingness*. In footnotes and in a few paragraphs at the end of the book he gives tantalizing hints as to how an ethics might be developed that is based on the ontology he works out there. In the footnotes he says that one can escape bad faith through a self-recovery of being in authenticity (BN 70) and alludes to "the possibility of an ethics of deliverance and salvation," that "can only be achieved after a radical conversion which we cannot discuss here" (BN 412). For, as he proclaims at the beginning of the closing section of the book entitled "Ethical Implications": "Ontology itself can not formulate ethical precepts" (BN 625). Nonetheless, he says that his analysis does provide a basis to reject the ethical position that he calls the spirit of seriousness, which posits values as existing independently of human consciousness. Such an ethics is a product of bad faith. Some people, he says next, have some inkling of this and so enact their bad faith only on a symbolic level. They "refrain from appropriating things for their own sake and try to realize the symbolic appropriation of their being-in-itself" (BN 627). It is hard to tell what Sartre means by this remark, but it is important to note that it is only for these people, those who get stuck somewhere between the spirit of seriousness and authenticity and fail to make the radical conversion he hints at in his footnote, that "all human activities are equivalent . . . and that all are on principle doomed to failure." It is only for these people that "it amounts to the same thing whether one gets drunk alone or is a leader of nations" (BN 627).

This last passage is perhaps the most misunderstood passage in all of *Being and Nothingness*. Many have assumed that it represents Sartre's own position and have seized on it to show that an ethics based on the ontology of *Being and Nothingness* is impossible. Although his plays of the period might imply that he believes that moral action is many times doomed to failure, Sartre does not take this position here. Someone for whom "it amounts to the same thing whether one gets drunk alone or is a leader of nations" still "shares in the spirit of seriousness" (BN 627). This person who rejects human ideals as meaningless seems similar to Beauvoir's figure of the nihilist. Sartre suggests here that there are other ways to fail to achieve authenticity besides bad faith that he does not elaborate on.

On the other hand, Sartre goes on, when the moral agent grasps, "that he is *the being by whom values exist* . . . his freedom will become conscious of itself and will reveal itself in anguish as the unique source of value and the nothingness by which the *world* exists" (BN 627). Presumably this is the insight on which authenticity would be based. Yet Sartre does not seem to be at all certain what will happen at this point. The rest of his ideas about ethics in this section are expressed in the form of questions. Most significantly for some later writers on Sartrean ethics, he asks, "is it possible for freedom to take itself for a value as the source of all value?" (BN 627). I will discuss the answers that can and have been given to this question later.

These few remarks in *Being and Nothingness* cannot stand in place of a fully worked out ethics; nor did Sartre intend them to. However, what Sartre says here mostly harmonizes with the approach that Beauvoir takes in *The Ethics of Ambiguity*. He suggests that to be moral one must come to grips with how human subjectivity is the source of all value and even the world itself. But note that Sartre says nothing about the role that other subjects play in this process or about our potential responsibilities to them.

"Existentialism is a Humanism"

Sartre does have something more substantive to say about how existentialism can serve as the foundation of an ethics in his lecture "Existentialism is a Humanism," subsequently published as a short book and then translated and widely distributed in the United States. Sartre gave this lecture on October 29, 1945 when existentialism had just caught the attention of the French public. The hall was packed. The book was printed in February 1946 and published that March by Nagel. Beauvoir was closely familiar with this text and had at least some input into the final form it took. Sartre apparently left the manuscript with her when he left Paris in December to visit his lover Dolorès in New York. Beauvoir wrote to him December 15 that she had "finished correcting" his lecture.[9] Almost certainly the text went straight from her pen to the publisher because Sartre did not return to Paris until March 15.[10] Of course, we do not know what changes she made. Sartre's biographer, Annie Cohen-Solal, reports that Sartre delivered the lecture without notes, although he followed an outline. Her description of what he said, culled from interviews with those who attended and newspaper reports, differs somewhat from the final printed version.[11] In a later interview Sartre says that the work contains ideas that were "not quite clearly formulated yet" or "completely focused." He intended only a few copies of it to be published. So many thousands were that it represents many people's only exposure to existentialism, which he saw as "a serious error."[12] Even so, the work is important just because so many have turned to it to see what an existentialist ethics would be like.

There are two places in this text where Sartre discusses the ethical implications of existentialism. First, towards the beginning he takes an approach that seems to be greatly influenced by Kant's moral thought. Kant says that we should act only on the maxim that we can at the same time will as a universal law. Sartre describes the individual as "a legislator choosing at the same time what humanity in its entirety should be."[13] To shrug off the question "What if everyone acted this way?" is to be in bad faith. In acting, the agent creates an image of what humans ought to be and do, an image "valid for all and for our entire epoch."[14]

Sartre's line of argument here is misguided. It does not jibe with his analysis of situation in *Being and Nothingness*. It is even inconsistent with some of the examples of moral choice that Sartre gives later in this same text. And, even if this approach to ethics were appropriate to existentialism, it would not get it very far. Assume that in acting I do create a model for all humankind to follow. What guarantees that it is the morally correct model? What if the images of humanity created by separate individuals, or even different actions by the same individual, conflict? Which one is to be preferred and why?

Sartre does give two examples at this point to support this idea that the agent, in choosing for himself or herself, is choosing for others too. The first example, that of a worker who chooses to join a Christian trade union rather than become a communist, works well. This choice does imply a judgment about what others should do. As Peter Caws points out, "It is true that there cannot be two different but opposing political solutions to the same problem in the same community. It is also true that there cannot be two true but incompatible global religions."[15] Secondly, Sartre asserts that even the decision to marry and have children is not solely an individual matter. In choosing marriage, one is "involving all humanity in monogamy."[16] But surely Sartre cannot mean that if I choose to marry and have children I think everyone should marry and have children. He must mean that this choice commits me to taking the position that marriage is a legitimate institution. This point might be better made by the reverse example: some people, although involved in heterosexual relationships very much the same as that of a married couple, choose not to get married, because it goes against their, for example, feminist convictions.

However, this Kantian idea that individual choice posits a universal ideal does not at all fit the examples of moral choice that Sartre gives later in "Existentialism is a Humanism." The case that Sartre discusses at greatest length, and the one that has most engaged the attention of commentators, is that of his student, a young man who has to decide between going away to join the forces of the Free French and staying to care for his aged sick mother. Sartre claims that there is nothing that he, or any ethical doctrine for that matter, can say to help him. At this point he does not exhort the young man to create an image of humanity valid for all through his choice. Rather he says: "You're free, choose, that is, invent."[17] By this I presume he means invent an original solution. Would the original solution the young man invents be the right one for everyone in his situation?

The example of moral choice that immediately follows is that of a young man Sartre knew when he was a prisoner of war who chose to become a Jesuit after a series of personal setbacks. Sartre implies that this choice is authentic because it sprang from the man's own interpretation of his past. But Sartre goes on to add that other interpretations were possible: "for example, that he might have done better to turn carpenter or revolutionary."[18] But if by his choice this man were creating a model for all humanity, it would make a great difference if he chose instead to become a carpenter or revolutionary.

Finally, Sartre also mentions two literary characters who make diametrically opposed choices in similar circumstances, that is, whether to resign themselves to the fact that the man they love is engaged to someone else. These "two strictly opposed moralities" are equivalent, he says, because each takes freedom as its goal.[19] But obviously someone who resigns herself in such a situation does not create a model valid for someone who chooses to disregard her lover's prior commitments and vice versa.

One could draw the conclusion from these examples that for Sartre sometimes there is not one right thing to do, or even that two opposed actions could both be right. In fact Sartre even says here that "one may choose anything if it is on the grounds of free engagement."[20] For this reason it is not surprising that some have charged that Sartre's existentialism leads to ethical subjectivism, that is, the position that a judgment that something is morally right or wrong is true only relative to the individual.[21] I will discuss later whether the same charge can be made against Beauvoir's ethics and, if so, what response can be made to it.

These three examples definitely do show, in any case, how a Kantian type of ethics that ties individual choice or action to universal standards that apply to everyone is at odds with an existentialist point of view. In commenting on the example of his student who must choose to leave or stay with his mother, Sartre suggests that values "are always too broad for the precise concrete case we are considering."[22] A universal approach to ethics cannot work because each concrete case is unlike any other. In *Being and Nothingness* Sartre discusses how a situation has both its objective and subjective aspects (which really cannot be distinguished from each other), because it is always *someone's* situation. Furthermore, everyone makes a different original choice of oneself, so each person's situation is unique. If so, then how can what I choose to do in my situation create a binding standard for how others should act in their own situations?

In "Existentialism is a Humanism" Sartre takes another approach to founding an existentialist ethics, one that has little or nothing to do with this first Kantian argument. People also bear a direct responsibility for the other people with whom they are actually engaged, he says. In order to identify the basis of this responsibility, Sartre first must discover a link between different subjects. This he claims to find revealed right from the beginning in Descartes's Cogito, which he borrows here as an indubitable starting point. Unlike Descartes, though, Sartre claims that "through the *I think* we reach our own self in the presence of the other and the other is just as real to us as our own selves."[23] Supporting this claim, Sartre says that one cannot be anything—cannot be, say, wicked or jealous—unless others recognize one to be so. Beauvoir makes a very similar argument in *Pyrrhus et Cinéas* but does not tie it to the Cartesian Cogito. It is a mistake for Sartre to do so, because in the Cogito one *is* precisely nothing, nothing but a thinking thing, that is. Sartre also says other things here that are reminiscent of things Beauvoir says in *Pyrrhus et Cinéas,* such as that I discover the other "as a freedom placed in front of me who thinks or wills only for or against me."[24]

The part of "Existentialism is a Humanism" that those concerned with ethics have paid the most attention to is where Sartre asserts that, contrary to what his critics charge, existentialism does allow one to pass judgments on others. One can bring both logical judgment and ethical judgment to bear on others' choices, he claims. First, it is simply not true that human actions are determined psychologically and thus not free. It is not true that values exist independently of the individual and impose themselves on him or her. The person who believes so, the person in bad faith, is in error. Of course, one can still choose to be in bad faith. But the only "strictly coherent attitude" is what Sartre calls here "good faith."[25]

Next Sartre tries to set up this logical judgment as the basis for making a moral judgment. If one avoids this error and accepts that values are not inscribed in the heavens but rather the creation of human freedom, then, Sartre claims, one wants or wills freedom for oneself and others. The argument that Sartre gives for this conclusion is very sketchy. The first step is his claim that "if man has once recognized that in his forlornness he imposes values, he can no longer will but one thing and that is freedom as the basis of all values." Furthermore, he goes on:

> in willing freedom we discover that it depends entirely on the freedom of others and that the freedom of others depends on ours. Of course, freedom as the definition of man does not depend on others, but as soon as there is involvement, I am obliged to will the freedom of others at the same time as I will my own freedom. I can take my freedom as a goal only if I take the freedom of others as a goal as well. Consequently, when in total authenticity I've recognized that man is the being in whom existence precedes essence, that he is a free being who, in various circumstances, can will only his freedom, I have at the same time recognized that I can will only the freedom of others.[26]

When Sartre refers to that freedom that is "the definition of man" I take him to be referring to ontological freedom, which he asserts does not depend on the freedom of others. But when this freedom engages itself in the world, the moral obligation arises to will the freedom of others as well as oneself, he says. His argument here bears unmistakable similarities to Beauvoir's argument in *The Ethics of Ambiguity* that "to will oneself free is also to will others free" (EA 73). Different conclusions can be drawn from these similarities. I will not discuss them here. In any case, in order to serve as the foundation of an ethics, this argument would need to be elaborated at much greater length. Furthermore, Sartre does not do very much with this idea. He does not use it to argue a commitment to liberation or to denounce oppression, as Beauvoir does. Instead he uses it only to condemn those in bad faith, whom he denounces as cowards and scum.

Also, it does not seem to have occurred to Sartre to ask why humans have to will themselves free or how they could want freedom above all, if they are already free, indeed condemned to be free, from the start. The ultimate meaning of acts of good faith is the quest for freedom in itself, he says. But how can, or why should humans quest after something they already have? As I showed in the last chapter, to answer these sorts of questions Beauvoir makes a distinction between ontological freedom and moral freedom.

Sartre certainly does address the issue of how existentialism can serve as a foundation for an ethics in "Existentialism is a Humanism." But what he says on this issue either leads to a dead end, as his Kantian argument does, or is radically undeveloped. His second line of argument—that to realize that values are the creation of human freedom leads one to want freedom for oneself and others—is promising, but raises questions that he does not even begin to address. Overall this work does not represent Sartre at his best. Full of bad arguments and hasty conclusions, it lacks the careful definition of terms and systematic exposition of *Being and Nothingness*.

Notebooks for an Ethics

Sartre's unpublished manuscripts on ethics, which have recently appeared in English translation under the title *Notebooks for an Ethics*, were written in 1947 and 1948, Sartre's literary executor reports, that is, after Beauvoir finished *The Ethics of Ambiguity*.[27] They represent Sartre's attempt to fulfill the promise he made in the closing pages of *Being and Nothingness* to devote a subsequent work to ethics.

Although he wrote an enormous amount, he apparently was not satisfied with it and ultimately dropped the project.[28] Thus these pages do not represent his long-awaited version of an existentialist ethics. The translator and editor of the English edition, who put a great deal of work into chasing down all of Sartre's obscure references in the work, judges it "a series of fragments rather than indicative of a final, systematic system."[29]

Nonetheless, it is full of fascinating analyses—phenomenological analyses in the style of Husserl—of types of behavior that have ethical significance: lying, violence, threats, demands, generosity. In it Sartre seems at first to have moved beyond his analysis of self-other relations in *Being and Nothingness*. In describing how a person responds to another's appeal he states, for instance: "I recognize the other's freedom without being pierced [by] a look."[30] He even describes the basis of this response very much in terms of Beauvoir's characterization of moral freedom in *The Ethics of Ambiguity*: it is to will "that the world have an infinity of finite futures each of which is directly projected by a free will and indirectly upheld by the willing of all the others, in that each wants the concrete freedom of the other."[31] Nonetheless, after a few more paragraphs he reverts to speaking of an "original conflict that has to first be surpassed."[32] Yet he nowhere indicates how this original conflict, presumably the conflict between self and other depicted in *Being and Nothingness*, can be or is surpassed.

Summary

As the closing pages of *Being and Nothingness* attest, Sartre himself seems to have felt a need to state how existentialism could serve as the basis for an ethics. His one effort to do so publically in his lecture "Existentialism is a Humanism" was not fully satisfactory, not even to him. He also was not satisfied with the manuscripts on ethics that he labored on after these two works. They do not at all resemble a finished work, in any case. For all these reasons, I conclude that something that can legitimately be called Sartre's existentialist ethics—that is, an ethics founded on the philosophy of *Being and Nothingness*—cannot be drawn from any of these sources, nor from all of them put together.

Sartrean Ethics

Some writers directly disagree with the above conclusion. They claim that Sartre does have an ethics or at least that the rudiments of an ethical theory can be found in his work.[33] Linda Bell, for instance, sees "a coherent and viable ethical position" to be implicit in Sartre's writings.[34] David Detmer also claims to find a "Sartrean" ethical theory there, even though it is necessary to "reconstruct" it.[35] Thomas Anderson, whose 1979 book began this school of interpretation, says that in his work Sartre "indicated the foundation and general structure of an ethics."[36] These three writers do not just make this claim; they go on to lay out the general precepts of this ethics, to supply arguments for them and to defend them against objections. I think that this is a very worthwhile project. It seems pointless to quibble over whether the ethics they describe deserves to be called Sartre's ethics, given the paucity of what he has to say on the subject. The way to bypass this controversy is simply to call this ethics Sartrean ethics, as these writers often do, rather than Sartre's ethics. Although Sartre may not have, these writers have developed an ethics that is consistently based on Sartre's ontology. While Sartre's ethics cannot, in my opinion, their Sartrean ethics *can* serve as another type of existentialist ethics against which to hold up Beauvoir's and compare it.

It did not occur to these writers to compare Beauvoir's ethics to Sartrean ethics, however. They assume that the ethics that Beauvoir describes in *The Ethics of Ambiguity* is Sartre's ethics. Indeed this is one reason they feel confident in attributing an ethics to Sartre. They assume that what she says is the same as what he would say.[37] So they often avail themselves of Beauvoir's arguments to support their positions. On this point I do insist on quibbling with them. In what follows I single out a number of ways that the position that Beauvoir takes in *The Ethics of Ambiguity* differs from the position they attribute to Sartre.

I have already discussed how Sartre does not have a conception of moral freedom as Beauvoir does. Thus when Sartre says in "Existentialism is a Humanism" that to be moral is to want freedom above all else, it does not make much sense because for him all humans are originally free and no one is more or less free than anyone else. Sartre does distinguish between ontological freedom and what these writers call concrete or practical freedom. Their handling of this

last issue—how someone can want something he or she already has—
hinges on this distinction. Whereas ontological freedom cannot be
increased, concrete freedom can be. So they interpret Sartre's talk of
a "quest for freedom as such" to involve a commitment to increasing
people's concrete freedom.[38]

It is true that Sartre says that the freedom to be quested after "is
willed in the concrete."[39] But there are at least two problems with
taking this tack. For one, Sartre also says that what the person in good
faith should want or will is "freedom as the foundation of all values."[40] The type of freedom that is the source of values is ontological
freedom, not concrete freedom. What connection can there be
between the realization that ontological freedom is the source of values and the obligation to increase humans' concrete freedom? More
broadly, to say that the goal of the person of good faith should be simply to increase humans' concrete freedom is not saying very much.
How much concrete freedom does any person deserve to have? What
if others' exercise of their concrete freedom impinges on mine? I deal
with some of these issues when I discuss how Beauvoir distinguishes
power from freedom in the next chapter. Here I will only repeat her
observation that "to be free is not to have the power to do anything
you want" (EA 91).

Except for Anderson, writers on Sartrean ethics do not take this
problem too seriously. They devote much more attention to another
problem they see to plague any attempt to base an ethics on freedom.
In their case, this problem springs from their decision to see freedom
as a *value*. In their reconstructions they all take as their beginning
point the question that Sartre poses himself at the end of *Being and
Nothingness*: "is it possible for freedom to take itself for a value as the
source of all values?" The answer, they see Sartre to be hinting, is yes.
Thus they see the ethical ideal of existentialism to be to move from
(1) the realization that freedom is the source of all values—a central
tenet of existentialism—to (2) choosing freedom to be one's ultimate
value. The problem they see lies in explaining what motivates this
transition. *Why* does realizing that freedom is the source of all values
lead one to take freedom as the highest value? Sartre appears to be
answering this question when he asserts in "Existentialism is a
Humanism" that "the attitude of strict consistency is that of good
faith."[41] Following Sartre's lead they have suggested that once one
sees that freedom is the source of all values logical consistency com-

pels one then to take freedom as the ultimate value. But this argument is in turn open to another objection. Why, since Sartre grounds all values in freedom, must one value logical consistency? Since all values are freely chosen one can choose just as readily not to value it.[42]

Some proponents of Sartrean ethics attempt to get around this objection by claiming that the inconsistency involved in not taking freedom as the highest value while at the same time recognizing that freedom is the source of all values is not logical inconsistency but rather some sort of practical or existential inconsistency.[43] The problem with this argument, as I see it, is that it does not square with the existentialist account of bad faith. According to this account I am driven to indulge in bad faith, to adopt the posture of the serious man, just because I *am* aware at some level that my values are self-chosen. Bad faith is a form of self-deception. It is only possible if I know what insight about myself I am trying to avoid. And bad faith is certainly not impossible in practice. For Sartre, at least, this is the moral posture of most of the people most of the time.

This last proposed solution to the problem of motivating the transition from recognizing that freedom is the source of all values to the choice of freedom as the ultimate value is related to another argument that has been singled out for making this move. Thomas Anderson, mistakenly I think, even ascribes this argument to Beauvoir. According to him the argument is: "since freedom is ontologically entailed in all values as their source, the choice of any and all values logically entails the prior valuing of freedom."[44] This argument is made in two different ways.

First, it can be interpreted as a type of Kantian transcendental argument that aims to identify freedom, which in this context means ontological freedom, as the condition of the possibility of valuing anything at all. But even if one accepts this argument, as it seems any good Sartrean must, why does it require one to take this freedom to be one's ultimate value? Again the argument boils down to an appeal to consistency, as Anderson recognizes: "To put it succinctly, if I do not value my freedom how could I consistently value any value it creates?"[45] But, again, the people who live in bad faith do not value their ontological freedom; they deny it exists. But they do value many things, for example, the things that their society or religion tells them are valuable. To charge these people with inconsistency does not seem very damning to me. Even if one accepts that one cannot coherently reject logical consistency as a value, it seems too slight a foundation to bear the weight of an entire moral theory.

Linda Bell brings another version of this argument into play, one which seems to have a better chance of getting somewhere. Like Anderson she argues: "Because freedom stands in a unique position of means to every choice, the choice of anything as a value logically entails the choice of freedom as a value."[46] She sees the connection between choosing anything as a value and choosing freedom as a value to be insured by the Kantian principle that one who wills the end wills the means. To reject this principle, she says, is logically incoherent: "The question, Why should one who chooses the end, will the means?, can have no answer except that willing the means is at least part of what is meant by willing the end."[47]

Actually there is a suppressed premise in Bell's argument. It is that if one values the end, then one values the means. The point she is trying to make by referring to the principle that to will the end is to will the means, I take it, is that human freedom is the means whereby any end at all is accomplished. Because it is the means by which any end is accomplished, if I value this end, I will value the means whereby I can bring it about. Thus in her argument Bell draws not on the Sartrean insight that human freedom is the source of all values, but rather the equally central insight that human freedom is the source of choice and action. It is this connection that she sees people in bad faith to be deceiving themselves about: "By willing, they exercise and thereby, at least implicitly, affirm the very freedom they endeavor to deny."[48] Without this suppressed premise that to value the end is to value the means, this seems to be an argument for convincing people that they are indeed free, not that they should make freedom their ultimate value.

But what does it mean to value freedom because it is the means to realizing anything else one may value? What type of freedom is meant here? What I have called in this chapter "concrete freedom" is the means whereby we realize particular ends. Does Bell intend her argument to convince people, especially those in bad faith, that they should value their concrete freedom? But the freedom that those in bad faith deny is their ontological freedom; they are as interested in increasing their concrete freedom as anyone else. Of course, ontological freedom is the source not only of value, but of all action. It is only because we have ontological freedom that we are able to engage in any goal-directed activity at all. So in this sense it is the means to any end. Should we value ontological freedom for this reason? Perhaps Bell's argument can be interpreted along these lines. Taken this way it seems to work, but only for people who do will an end. It would not be convincing to Beauvoir's sub-man or Camus's stranger, for instance.[49]

The problem of explaining why people should take freedom as their ultimate value only arises if one sees this idea as central to, even the basis of, an existentialist ethics, as these writers on Sartrean ethics do. Although a similar problem confronts Beauvoir's ethics, as I will soon explain, this particular one does not. For Beauvoir does not talk about freedom being a value in *The Ethics of Ambiguity* as Sartre does in *Being and Nothingness*. Granted, there is a passage where she seems to be headed in this direction. The first three sentences are even quoted by writers on Sartrean ethics to support the position they attribute to Sartre, perhaps because the parallels between this passage and the passage from "Existentialism is a Humanism" where Sartre states that the ethical person wants "freedom as the basis of all values" are striking. Here she says:

> Freedom is the source from which all significations and all values spring. It is the original condition of all justification of existence. The man who seeks to justify his life must want freedom itself absolutely and above everything else. At the same time that it requires the realization of concrete ends, of particular projects, it requires itself universally. It is not a ready-made value which offers itself from the outside to my abstract adherence, but it appears (not on the plane of facility, but on the moral plane) as a cause of itself. It is necessarily summoned up by the values which it sets up and through which it sets itself up. It cannot establish a denial of itself, for in denying itself, it would deny the possibility of any foundation. To will oneself moral and to will oneself free are one and the same decision. (EA 24)

Beauvoir's reasoning in this passage is not easy to follow. But it is clear what the conclusion she thinks she is arguing for is. It is not that we should make freedom our ultimate value; it is that we should will ourselves free.

Beauvoir does seem to conceive of freedom as a value in an important passage in *The Blood of Others*. But the stance she appears to take there can be criticized from the standpoint she takes in *The Ethics of Ambiguity*. At the end of the novel Blomart justifies his decision to send his Resistance fighters on another sabotage mission by appealing to the "supreme good" of freedom, "that good which saves each man from all the others and from [himself]" (BO 292). To make freedom into a supreme good in this way seems to turn existentialist ethics into a strange sort of utilitarianism. Furthermore, in appealing to freedom as the supreme good Blomart invites comparison to the serious man whom Beauvoir condemns in *The Ethics of Ambiguity* for elevating a value, which like all values has its source in human freedom, to the level of an absolute and using it as a justification for sacrificing human lives.

In other places Beauvoir refers to freedom not as a value but as an end, "the only end capable of justifying men's undertakings."[50] But freedom as an end is not a static goal; it is rather "nothing else but precisely the free movement of existence" (EA 29). The freedom we should aim at as an end is moral freedom. It involves a certain way of living our lives. In *The Ethics of Ambiguity* Beauvoir conceives of freedom not as a value, but rather as a state or condition—ontological freedom as the state of all humans and moral freedom as the state fully realized by only a few. Thus when Beauvoir says that to justify one's life one must want freedom absolutely and above everything else, she means that the ethical person attempts to achieve this state.

Because writers on Sartrean ethics do not have a conception of moral freedom, they are driven to conceive of freedom as a value. If freedom is a state or a condition, it does not make sense for them to say that the moral person quests after freedom, since all humans are originally free. It does make sense, by contrast, to hold that the moral person values his or her ontological freedom whereas the unethical person does not. (As Thomas Anderson puts it, the existentialists "call for man to value the freedom that is his very structure."[51]) For, as Sartre's account of bad faith lays out, one can choose to react to the basic fact of one's ontological freedom in different ways—to give it a positive or a negative value.

Why Pursue Moral Freedom?

Beauvoir does not have to come up with an argument to convince people to accept freedom as the highest value, because she does not see freedom as a value, in *The Ethics of Ambiguity*, at least. However, a similar challenge faces her ethics—that of convincing people that they should pursue moral freedom. And it seems she does not surmount that challenge. She provides arguments to show that if I seek to realize my own moral freedom, I must work to further the moral freedom of others, since my moral freedom is intertwined with theirs. But she provides no argument to convince me that I should seek moral freedom in the first place. Indeed even if she or someone else could provide a logically compelling argument why I should seek moral freedom, I could always choose not to accept it. I could choose not to be logical. This is the same objection made against those who appeal to logical consistency to motivate the move from seeing freedom as the source of value to accepting freedom as the ultimate value in Sartrean ethics.

My strategy in dealing with this objection is simply to cede the field. As I see it, nothing can compel me or anyone else to seek moral freedom. My free choice alone commits me to this pursuit. On this point I agree with Anderson: "both Sartre and de Beauvoir explicitly admit that logic and reason themselves have value only if man chooses them to."[52] Beauvoir says only that the person who wants to justify his or her life must want moral freedom. This leaves the question open: why seek to justify one's life?

Beauvoir does say that humans have a deep need to justify their life: "Moral anxiety does not come to man from without; he finds within himself the anxious question, 'What's the use?' Or, to put it better, he himself is this urgent interrogation. He flees it only by fleeing himself, and as soon as he exists he answers" (EA 72). Beauvoir is not saying that humans *must* justify their lives. She is just making the phenomenological observation that humans do feel the need to do so. Certainly people can choose not to fulfill needs that they have, even their deepest needs. Another answer that Beauvoir gives to the "why be moral?" question is that it is in one's self-interest to: "It may perhaps be said that it is for *himself* that he is moral" (EA 72). Certainly the way that she describes the life of moral freedom it is more fulfilling than the life of the sub-man or nihilist. But one can always choose not to do what is in one's self-interest.

On this issue it is very helpful to turn to what the noted Sartre scholar Hazel Barnes wrote in her book on existentialist ethics published in 1967:

the initial choice to be ethical always stands outside any particular ethics. It is never possible to take a principle which a philosophical system has established

in response to the challenge to be ethical and then seek to use it as a categorical imperative to compel the original choice to be ethical. Existentialism
is not unique in this respect. It has merely emphasized what other philosophies have tended to ignore.[53]

According to this line of reasoning, the efforts of writers on Sartrean
ethics to come up with an argument for taking freedom as the ultimate value are doomed from the start. Once one has made the choice
to be ethical, then arguments can be offered as to which ethical system one should adopt, as Barnes sees it, although "irrational" factors
also enter in.[54] However, if one chooses not to be ethical then no
argument of any ethical theory is compelling. She, like Beauvoir,
though, holds that the choice to be ethical springs out of a deep
human need and brings psychological satisfaction.[55]

To illustrate what a choice not to be ethical is like Barnes uses
Dostoevsky's character of the Underground Man: "the Underground Man asserts that he prizes his freedom not to be ethical. He
does not have to justify himself, he is not obliged to choose happiness or any other self-evident good. He chooses his independence of
all regulating value systems."[56] The Underground Man exercises his
ontological freedom in the same way that Beauvoir's nihilist or
Camus's stranger does, by refusing all values, but he is more willful
and articulate.

She also recognizes that his case presents a challenge to the
dichotomy between authentic and inauthentic choice that Sartre
seems to set up as a moral standard. For the Underground Man cannot be charged with inauthenticity. He can even be said to have done
what writers on Sartrean ethics argue for and made freedom his ultimate value! Barnes says,

> the Underground Man is fully aware that he and he alone is responsible for
> what he chooses. Indeed it is freedom itself which he chooses as the value so
> far beyond all others that he pits it against all possible values which might in
> the future result from submitting this freedom to any sort of calculated
> restriction, external or internal.[57]

The Underground Man makes his ontological freedom his ultimate
and only value.

Barnes's analysis of the Underground Man leads her to propose
that a person has three major ethical stances from which to choose.
First, one can choose to be unethical by celebrating one's ontological

freedom by self-consciously rejecting all standards whatsoever except one's fleeting personal whim. Although an authentic realization of one's freedom, this choice is unsatisfactory in all other regards. Alternatively, the realization of the dizzying extent of one's freedom can lead not to the perverse pride of the Underground Man but rather to anguish, despair, or Heideggerian angst, which drives one to run from one's freedom in bad faith. This is the scenario Sartre depicts in *Being and Nothingness* and much of his literary work. This choice is an inauthentic one, because it denies it is a choice. However, whether it is a choice of the ethical or the unethical is hard to say. These people do recognize and act on their need to justify their lives. But they justify their lives by means of value systems that deny their freedom. Recognizing their need to justify their lives leads them to lie to themselves. Thus they occupy a territory somewhere between the ethical and the non-ethical.[58]

Thirdly, there is the choice to be ethical, which is also an authentic choice: one justifies one's life by choosing to take full responsibility for one's values and actions. This choice sounds like the choice to will oneself free that both Sartre and Beauvoir refer to. But for Barnes to choose to be ethical is not equivalent to choosing to accept any one ethical system, although a true commitment to justify one's life generates certain general standards that any satisfactory system of ethics must meet. Above all, it must upon reflection be seen to lead to a way of life that holds the most value for the person concerned. In comparison, by choosing to reject all values, the Underground Man chooses to live a life that has no value for him in order to show that he is free to reject any value.

Once one has made an initial choice to be ethical, presumably, one can be convinced by the arguments made by proponents of existentialist ethics, Beauvoir included, to adopt their ethics. But Barnes's position entails that the choice to be a Kantian or a utilitarian, for instance, is an authentic choice too. It is thus up to existentialists to provide better reasons to adopt their point of view. The choice to live in bad faith is not an authentic choice. Yet I think that the person who makes this choice can no more be convinced by arguments to be authentically ethical than can the Underground Man. If you initially choose to deceive yourself, that is, hold as true what is not true, no argument can convince you of the truth. You have chosen not to accept the truth. You first have to choose not to deceive yourself in order to allow yourself to be convinced by any arguments.

What those who labor away constructing arguments to convince anyone, for example, to take freedom as the ultimate value forget is that if there were some overwhelmingly convincing reason for people to be moral, we could not then explain why so many people are not moral. People who like myself live in relatively safe bourgeois communities tend to view violence and dispossession as an anomaly—as an affront to the rational order, which in a way they are. But even a cursory review of human history or a glance at the evening newspaper reveals the astonishing range of evil humans are capable of. Recent incidents of school violence in the U.S. show that appalling things happen even in comfortable bourgeois communities. How can children do such things, people wail, and look everywhere to find causes for such behavior. The existentialist answer is that nothing *causes* them to act that way; they are free and choose to (and have access to the relevant instruments of destruction). For this reason only existentialism leaves room for the full scope of human wrongdoing according to Beauvoir: "Existentialism alone gives—like religion—a real role to evil" (EA 34).

Beauvoir gives reasons why one should pursue moral freedom. For one, it fulfills a deep human need we have to justify our lives. Furthermore, the joint projects we engage in with others enrich our lives. But she offers no philosophical argument to convince us that we should seek moral freedom. Adopting Barnes's reasoning for my own purposes, I contend that she cannot. But in this regard her ethics is no more deficient than is any other ethics. There is no philosophical argument that can decisively convince people to be moral. Philosophy has been on the scene for a long time. Philosophers as far back as Socrates have engaged themselves with this issue. If an overwhelmingly convincing argument were available, one would think it would have occurred to someone by now.

Existentialist Ethics and Ethical Subjectivism

Now I will discuss whether Beauvoir's ethics is open to the charge that existentialist views about freedom and value commit it to a form of ethical subjectivism. To do so I will first consider whether criticisms that have been directed against Sartre—specifically the charge that existentialism cannot serve as a suitable basis for an ethics because of his views on freedom and values—also apply to Beauvoir. The charges that have been brought against Sartre's existentialism in this regard fall into two different camps, those that condemn existentialist views about freedom and those that condemn existentialist views about value, although they are often confused with each other.

The first charge is that, since existentialism bases ethics on freedom, it offers no criterion with which to distinguish right and wrong actions. The second charge is that given existentialism's credo that values are the creation of human freedom any criterion that can be used to distinguish wrong actions from right actions is subjective. Actions simply have the values that agents and observers apply to them, for there is no standpoint external to the individual from which these values can be surveyed. Neither is there a vantage point from which to adjudicate moral conflicts. The first charge, that according to existentialism ethical judgments are not possible at all, is much more devastating. The second criticism recognizes that ethical judgments are possible according to existentialism—indeed they are the source of moral value for it—but questions the legitimacy of these judgments. I will show decisively that Beauvoir's ethics is not open to the first charge; it is even questionable whether Sartre is. It is less clear-cut whether Beauvoir's ethics is open to the second charge, as I will discuss. But even if it is, I will show, Beauvoir's position does not lead to some of the alarming consequences that some people think ethical subjectivism does.

A number of critics have charged that Sartre's intention to base ethics on freedom commits him to the position that any action that is freely chosen is moral. But this position, they object, leads to ridiculous consequences. For instance, Mary Warnock writes: "If choosing freely for oneself is the highest value, the free choice to wear red socks is as valuable as the free choice to murder one's father or sacrifice oneself for one's friend."⁵⁹ Actually, this position, if it were Sartre's, would lead to the consequence that it is impossible to make moral judgments. Remember that for Sartre every act is equally free in terms of ontological freedom: he says that we are condemned to be free and the slave is as free as the master. Thus for Sartre, *if* every action that is freely chosen is moral, then no action is immoral. But if no action is immoral, it makes no sense to talk about morality at all. Alvin

Plantinga, who sees Sartre to be committed to this position, objects along these lines: "But morality presupposes that . . . there is the possibility of right and wrong. . . . This doctrine makes negative moral judgments impossible and positive ones otiose."[60]

David Detmer, who includes an in-depth treatment of ethical subjectivism in his book on Sartrean ethics, points out how Sartre's existentialism can be defended from this objection. Sartre does offer a criterion with which to judge an agent's action that is independent of the agent's own appraisal of the action: whether it is done in bad faith or not. Whereas in *Being and Nothingness* Sartre says that good faith seeks to take refuge in being,[61] in "Existentialism is a Humanism" he holds up good faith or authenticity as the moral ideal.[62] From what Sartre says in "Existentialism is a Humanism" one can conclude that one acts in good faith when one recognizes that one's actions are freely chosen on the basis of freely chosen values and thus takes full responsibility for them. Many people do not do this and on the basis of this criterion they can be judged to be acting immorally.

However, as Detmer himself points out, this defense is open to two further objections. First, critics have charged that Sartre is not even entitled to this moral standard. Here is one point where this first charge made against Sartre's existentialism is connected to the second charge of ethical subjectivism. If all values are freely chosen, why must I put a positive value on good faith? Could I not choose instead to approve of self-deception in general or at least regard it as benign when I see others indulging in it? (Accepting my own self-deception would be tricky, however. I would first have to admit to myself that I am deceiving myself in order to accept it, in which case I would no longer be deceiving myself.) Sartre appears to be arguing in "Existentialism is a Humanism" that deceiving oneself about the extent of one's freedom and the nature of values in particular involves not only a logical but a moral error. But it certainly can be questioned whether this argument succeeds.

Critics object further that even if this moral standard of acting in good faith is justified, it is not enough to rule out actions that most people—all writers on ethics at least—would judge to be immoral. To illustrate this objection Detmer gives the example of the authentic torturer: "A torturer who candidly says, 'I have freely chosen to kidnap and torture you, and I take full responsibility for my choice,' is apparently above criticism, according to Sartre's theory."[63] Indeed the figure of the cold-blooded villain is a staple of popular culture. One could question of course how many people like this really exist; most actual wrongdoers when confronted come up with many excuses for their actions. Nonetheless, even if there are only a few (like the Nazi general Hermann Goering, for instance), this objection still holds. Besides, it points to a more basic problem with singling out bad faith as the defining feature of immoral actions. Most people think that it is what the person does, not his or her attitude towards it, that makes an action immoral.

I have gone into these objections at some length because I want to show that the existentialist ethics that Beauvoir sketches out in *The Ethics of Ambiguity* is not open to any of them. For one thing, nothing that Beauvoir says in this text commits her to a position that it is impossible to make moral judgments. She does not hold that any action that is freely chosen is moral. Beauvoir bases her ethics on freedom: as an existentialist there is nothing else for her to base it on. But she distinguishes between ontological freedom and moral freedom. For her only acts that are free in this second sense are moral. Secondly, Beauvoir does use the concept of bad faith, although not exactly in the same way that Sartre does. Bad faith for her is not consistent with moral freedom. But forgoing self-deception is not sufficient by itself to attain moral freedom either. Beauvoir's ethics sets up an additional requirement that must be fulfilled: one must act to defend and develop the moral freedom of oneself and others. The actions of the authentic torturer obviously fail to meet this standard. In fact torture definitely diminishes moral freedom. It is often practiced by repressive regimes to inhibit the willingness of people to resist oppression. As I have already discussed, Beauvoir does not have an argument to convince even the most recalcitrant that they should seek moral freedom. But there is no reason why she is not justified in adopting moral freedom as the moral ideal of her ethics. It does not contradict or otherwise transgress the central tenets of her existentialism. Indeed her argument, as I will soon explore, is that it follows closely upon them.

Now to turn to the more difficult question of whether Beauvoir's ethics reduces in the end to a form of ethical subjectivism. This question is related to the second charge brought against Sartre that for him actions can be judged to be right and wrong, but these judgments are all subjective, that is, true only to the one making them.

The reason that critics have claimed that Sartre's ontology leads to ethical subjectivism is because of his thesis about the ontological status of values. Indeed Sartre himself seems to make such a connection in one passage in *Being and Nothingness*:

> Values in actuality are demands which lay claim to a foundation. But this foundation can in no way be *being*. . . . Value derives its being from its exigency and not its exigency from its being . . . it can be revealed only to an active freedom which makes it exist as value by the sole fact of recognizing it as such. It follows that my freedom is the unique foundation of values and that *nothing*, absolutely nothing, justifies me in adopting this or that particular value, this or that particular scale of values. As a being by whom values exist, I am unjustifiable. (BN 38)

Here Sartre seems to conclude that it follows from the fact that values are the creation of human freedom that there is no justification for adopting any particular value or set of values. However, Sartre nowhere says that we therefore should refrain from making moral judgments. (Critics have pointed out that he himself issued many moral pronouncements and urged others to do so as *engagé* intellectuals.) So Sartre's thesis about values seems only to have implications for the status of moral judgments. His position thus comes close to ethical subjectivism, which is, under one definition: "a theory according to which moral judgments about men or their actions are judgments about the way people react to these men and actions—that is, the way they think or feel about them."[64]

Beauvoir holds the same thesis about the origin and ontological status of values as Sartre does. In the passage I quoted earlier she states: "Freedom is the source from which all significations and all values spring. It is the original condition of all justification of existence" (EA 24). But in this passage she uses this thesis to argue for something quite different from what Sartre argues for in the passage from *Being and Nothingness* I just quoted. She does not assert that because all values spring from human freedom, there is no justification for adopting any value or value system. Rather she argues that, since freedom is the source of all justification, if you want to justify your life you must justify it through freedom. You must will yourself free, which for her is equivalent to adopting a moral point of view. Thus the fact that freedom is the source of all value and justification is for her a reason that one should justify one's life by trying to be moral, not a reason to conclude that no action is justifiable. Her position is that freedom makes certain demands on a person. If you choose to meet these demands you must submit to certain requirements. That is why existentialist ethics "does not lead to the anarchy of personal whim. Man is free; but he finds his law in his very freedom" (EA 156).

However, although Beauvoir does not outwardly embrace ethical subjectivism as Sartre seems to in this passage from *Being and Nothingness*, could not her position still end up equivalent to it in the end? The question remains: what does justify any particular moral judgment for Beauvoir? How can I know, for example, that I am right to conclude that a certain action advances the cause of moral freedom? In the last section of *The Ethics of Ambiguity* Beauvoir describes how difficult it is to know what the right thing to do is sometimes, particularly in the context of political action. But she offers a method to use to face these difficulties and, as I will soon discuss, does render judgment, even in difficult cases. Nevertheless, she holds that we can never know for sure that we are doing the right thing. To admit to such doubt is even a sign that one is on the side of moral freedom: "morality resides in the painfulness of an indefinite questioning . . . what distinguishes the tyrant from the man of good will is that the first rests in the certainty of his aims, whereas the second keeps asking himself, 'Am I really working for the liberation of men?'" (EA 133). The influence of Kierkegaard is apparent here. In her memoirs she reports: "I had been very struck by Kierkegaard's idea that a *genuinely* moral person could never have an easy conscience."[65]

It seems that Beauvoir must be classified as being at least in the subjectivist camp. For her, "It is human existence which makes values spring up in the world" (EA 15). She would never claim that actions, or even some actions, are objectively right or wrong in the sense that they are right or wrong independently of and in abstraction from any possible human judgments about them. She seems to share the conviction that Bernard Williams identifies as lying at the heart of the subjectivist position: "that there is no moral order 'out there'."[66]

But Williams himself provides an argument to show that a philosophically rigorous ethical subjectivism does not lead to the alarming consequences that some think that it does. He takes the example of a man protesting what he sees as a monstrous political injustice. When converted to ethical subjectivism the man begins to doubt his stance, asking after all who is *he* to say that the perpetrators are wrong? Williams points out that such doubt is not called for by ethical subjectivism. It comes from

> importing the idea that there is such a thing as objective rightness, only he is not sure whether these other people's actions possess it or not. Sticking to the subjectivist path, he must recognize that if he chooses to think they are wrong and that he is right in protesting, then no one can say he is wrong either.[67]

This man's doubt whether he is actually right and they are wrong is not anchored by his own convictions; it inhabits what Williams calls a "mid-air place" hovering above the value systems of both the man and the people he is protesting, which is a vantage point that does not exist according to ethical subjectivism. This is not to say that ethical subjectivism—or existentialist ethics—rules out one having doubts that one's moral judgments are correct. Someone can doubt his or her moral judgment for many reasons. The subjectivist is just barred, according to this argument, from having moral doubts for philosophical reasons.

This same argument applies to Beauvoir's ethics. A conviction that all values are the creation of human freedom does not give one good reason to doubt that his or her moral judgments are correct. Thus her thesis about the ontological status of values does not lead by itself to the consequence that no one is entitled to the conviction that one's moral judgments ultimately are correct. If this were a conclusion that followed from her position, it would certainly undercut it.

Furthermore, I want to argue, one is as entitled to one's moral convictions according to Beauvoir's existentialist ethics as one is in any other ethical system. I said before that Beauvoir holds that we can never know for sure if what we think is the morally right thing to do really is the morally right thing to do. And this is not just because we are always confined to the present moment in making our choices and thus have limited knowledge. Rather, even looking back on the past, in possession of all the relevant information, we sometimes wonder if we made the right choice. What I want to ask is whether a moral objectivist, someone who strenuously asserts that values and standards have force independently of human awareness of them, is entitled to claim that he or she can know for sure in all cases—or even any case—that his or her moral judgments are correct. According to an objectivist point of view, there is a standard "out there" that one can use to match one's actual moral judgments up to. But what guarantees that any particular person has access to this realm and can perceive this standard? Certainly the ethical objectivist, like the adherent of existentialist ethics, like us all, thinks that many people's moral judgments are not correct. He or she thinks that many people think that something is morally right when it is actually morally wrong and vice versa. Indeed since people hold conflicting moral views, some of them must be incorrect. But what guarantees for the ethical objectivist that one's own moral judgments fall into the category of correct moral judgments and not the other category? Of course one can give arguments, give reasons for one's position. But what makes these arguments and reasons decisive? In any case, according to objectivism someone's moral judgments are correct not because of these arguments or for these reasons, but because they make use of the correct values or bring the correct standards to bear, those values and standards that have force independent of human perception of them.

Granted, the locus of uncertainty is different in either case. For objectivist ethics, when I am asking myself which thing is the right thing to do, there is (usually, at least) a guaranteed correct answer. The question, however, is how I know for sure that the answer that I come up with is the correct answer. For Beauvoir's existentialist ethics this problem does not arise. There is nothing that transcends human experience that I must struggle to know. Instead I am unsure whether the thing that I chose to do, or chose to regard as the right thing for others to do, *is* the morally right thing to do. There is simply not a guaranteed correct answer to this question. However, in the end what difference does this difference make either to the experience of moral uncertainty or to its outcome?

The same strategy can be used in answering the charge that an ethical subjectivist position is unsatisfactory because it offers no vantage point from which to adjudicate conflicting moral judgments. An objectivist ethics, on the other hand, the reasoning goes, leaves room for a perspective from which one moral judgment can be seen to be right and the conflicting judgments declared to be wrong. My response is that, yes, one judgment would be definitely wrong according to this point of view. But the question again is how I can know for sure which one it is. If someone told a dyed-in-the-wool objectivist that a firmly held moral conviction of hers was wrong according to objective standards, would not she be likely to respond that this person was in error, that on the contrary her judgment was right according to objective standards and this person was wrong. I do not see how moral objectivism rules out or even diminishes conflict between people over moral issues.

I conclude for these reasons that an objectivist moral theory has no advantage over a subjectivist one as far as establishing moral certainty is concerned. That it holds out the abstract possibility of moral certainty does not make much of a difference in terms of the actual experience of moral conflicts. There is one further criticism, however, that philosophers who are unhappy with the prospect of ethical subjectivism make. This perceived deficiency even seems to be the real source of their dissatisfaction with it. Bernard Williams, for instance, complains, "the reason why even defused subjectivism seems to have left something out is that moral thinking *feels* as though it mirrored something, as though it were constrained to follow, rather than be freely creative."[68] David Detmer likewise appeals to the phenomenology of moral experience in rejecting what he sees to be Sartre's subjectivism: "I *discover*, in many cases without it in any way depending on any particular project of mine, that certain people are 'courageous,' while others are 'cowardly,' that some acts are 'kindly,' while others are 'cruel'."[69] To discover these features means they exist in some sense prior to our discovery of them.

I do not necessarily disagree with these descriptions of moral experience. I just question whether they have the philosophical import that these authors seem to think they do. For instance, writers of fiction report how they come to discover aspects of their characters' personality during the process of writing about them. Yet no one would want to claim that the personality traits of fictional characters exist "out there" somewhere before these characters are created—that they exist independently of this process of creation. There might be something about the nature of moral experience that compels us to make the judgments we do, or to feel compelled to make the judgments we do. But might not this feeling of compulsion derive from the nature of the experience itself, rather than from the nature of what is experienced?

Existentialist Ethics and Moral Dilemmas

Sartre makes a similar point in "Existentialism is a Humanism" when discussing the case of his student who is deciding whether to run away and join the Free French or stay and care for his ailing mother. He says: "No general ethics can show what is to be done."[70] Christian ethics and Kantian ethics both offer rules that might help the student decide, but these rules can generate opposing answers depending on how they are applied. The Kantian dictum that one should never treat another simply as a means is not decisive. If he leaves he is failing to treat his mother as an end. If he stays he is treating the other soldiers as a means. It is not Kantian ethics that determines what to do, but rather the choice he makes of how to apply the categorical imperative. Any appeal to objective standards or values operates much the same way. It is not the standards or values that determine what one should do, but rather one's choice of which standards and values apply, along with one's choice of how to apply them. Seen this way any moral judgment in the end is an "invention."

David Detmer interprets Sartre's use of this example of the student to be an argument for ethical subjectivism. According to him, Sartre wants to show that we do not know the right thing to do in this case because there is no right thing to do. He then sees Sartre generalizing from this case to conclude that in all cases of moral choice there is no right thing to do, so we have to "invent" one every time. If this were Sartre's argument it would be a very poor one. As Judith Jarvis Thompson points out, "It is a good question why people suppose that there are no answers to moral questions unless it is easy to find them all out."[71]

According to my interpretation, Sartre is arguing for something else, his conclusion I quoted earlier that "no general ethics can show what is to be done." The point is that no matter what ethical principles one appeals to, all moral decisions end up being a matter of free personal choice. Of course, I am also interpreting Sartre's argument here to be an argument for ethical subjectivism—or more properly speaking, a defense of it—but a different and I hope a better one.

In her essay "Idéalisme moral et réalisme politique" Beauvoir mentions how French collaborators in the Vichy government appealed in their war crimes trials to "grand eternal maxims" like the patriotic duty to serve one's country to excuse their actions. Beauvoir points out that these maxims do not specify what it means to serve one's country. The collaborators said that they wanted the best for France, but the France their actions served was not "our France," Beauvoir asserts (IMRP 53). Peace, justice, and order are important values, but what sort of peace, what sort of justice, what order should we value?

I do not mean to suggest that general ethical principles can justify collaboration with a brutal invading army just as readily as they can justify any other course of action. I think that Beauvoir would agree that the excuses given by the collaborators are prime examples of bad faith. Elsewhere in this essay Beauvoir recognizes that general ethical principles do rule out certain actions. As David Detmer points out, in the case of Sartre's student, the options he is struggling to choose among do not include murdering his mother or joining up with the Nazis.[72] Beauvoir argues that while ethical principles might limit what it is morally permissible to do, they cannot determine exactly what should be done: "general and abstract precepts of morality can only limit the field of political action without helping to find the solution to the specific problems that it poses" (IMRP 53).

What is the significance of moral dilemmas such as the one confronting Sartre's student for Beauvoir's existentialist ethics? It is the same as for any other system of ethics. They are cases where it is very hard to decide what the right thing to do is. I said before that Beauvoir sees a certain amount of uncertainty to dog any sincere attempt one makes to be moral. But I argued that it does not follow that she, or any other proponent of existentialist ethics, is not entitled to firm moral convictions. Moral uncertainty or even moral doubt does not lead to nihilism. To apply the statement from Thompson I quoted earlier in a different context: it is wrong for critics of existentialist ethics to "suppose that there are not answers to any moral questions unless it is easy to find out what all of them are."[73]

Beauvoir's Criteria for Personal Moral Choice

Nowhere in *The Ethics of Ambiguity*, however, does Beauvoir refer to an apparently unresolvable moral dilemma like the one confronting Sartre's student. She mentions a number of tough moral decisions concerning others, but in each case tells us what she thinks the right thing to do is. I will go through each of the four examples she uses, supplying a justification for her decision drawn from her general characterization of existentialist ethics in each case.

First, Beauvoir gives the example of a young girl who, saved from a suicide attempt, goes on to get married, have children, be happy. Her friends were right to enable this girl subsequently to reject "this heedless act," she judges. The distinction that she makes between ontological and moral freedom allows her to avoid the overly rigorous position that one may never intercede in the decisions of others. While undoubtedly a free act, this girl's suicide attempt was not an exercise of moral freedom. In it she was not acting in common with others to pursue a joint end. Yet she is certainly capable of doing so. By saving her life her friends were enabling her to act not just freely, but so that her end might be freedom.

Against this example Beauvoir balances the example of the melancholic patient who is thwarted in his recurrent suicide attempts by the cheerful tyrants controlling his care. The implication is that they are wrong to stand in his way. A more problematic example that Beauvoir gives is that of an addicted friend desperately begging for money to support his habit. Such an individual ideally should be made aware of the "real demands of his freedom" (EA 136), the demands of moral freedom, in order to seek a cure. But if one can do nothing to bring about such a conversion, one might as well give in to his pleas, she says. At this point, Beauvoir turns consequentialist. If denied, the addict might resort to truly desperate measures. In opposition to Kant she adds: "It is no more necessary to serve an abstract ethics obstinately than to yield without due consideration to impulses of pity or generosity; violence is justified only if it opens concrete possibilities to the freedom which I am trying to save" (EA 136–37).

Beauvoir also appeals to this last criterion, whether intervention in someone's life holds out real hope to him or her, in a fourth case, the case depicted in Ibsen's *The Wild Duck*:

> An individual lives in a situation of falsehood; the falsehood is violence, tyranny: shall I tell the truth in order to free the victim? It would first be necessary to create a situation of such a kind that the truth might be bearable and that, though losing his illusions, the deluded individual might again find about him reasons for hoping. (EA 143)

There is one factor that can explain why Beauvoir takes the position she does in each of these four cases. The key lies in whether an act works to open up a future for the person involved. Saving a young and healthy person from suicide does open up a future, or at least keeps a future open that would otherwise be closed. Keeping a terminally ill or chronically incapacitated person from committing suicide, on the other hand, is not an act that opens up a future, because due to that person's situation the future is closed off. It is not just a matter of the number of years left to live or even the quality of life to be expected during those years, but more of the opportunities that those years will offer. And these opportunities cannot be measured in terms of impersonal criteria. According to Beauvoir's conception of temporality the future only exists as the future of a distinct individual or group of individuals.

But the criteria used to judge what the future offers cannot be wholly subjective either. To the young girl who attempts suicide the future looks hideously bleak. But since her life is intertwined with others, her actual future, with its distinct concrete possibilities, intersects and is embedded in the future of these other people. They thus hold a good vantage point from which to judge her assessment of the future wrong.

In the case of the drug addict, his future is a matter of much more uncertainty than the incapacitated patient or even the young girl. Only he can choose to open up a future for himself that contains real possibilities for free action by seeking a cure; his friend by denying him the money for drugs cannot force him to do so. So the friend can only take into account the addict's immediate future, the next day or hours, which given the addict's situation remains very volatile. The friend may be justified in giving him money just to forestall disaster in this period. Remember that Beauvoir is not arguing here that one has an obligation to supply the addict with funds. Nor does her argument rule out the possibility that one may be justified in deciding that giving in to him is unwise because it might join his future to one's own, thus incurring responsibilities that one does not choose to take on.

In the example of deciding whether to tell the truth to a person whose whole life is set up on the basis of an illusion, this is a case where, according to Beauvoir's viewpoint, the truth does not necessarily set one free. To tell the truth to a person completely unprepared for it would be to open a future for him in one sense: it would be to introduce a wholly new future completely severed from the past and the present. But the important question is whether this future would be one containing what Beauvoir calls concrete possibilities for the person involved. Normally, due to the nature of human temporality, the future is always of a piece with the present and the past. Action, to be meaningful, must be anchored in this continuum. By robbing someone of all his illusions in one fell swoop, one explodes this person's past, floats his future out of reach, and turns the present into a knife's edge. This is not to say that people do not sometimes receive shocks of this sort, due to historical events, say, and go on to survive them. The point is that it is cruel for one person to play this role in another person's life. If one intervenes in a person's life like this, one has a responsibility to engage oneself in the whole of that life.

The relation that one's own actions have to another person's future, then, is the crucial issue in deciding what to do when faced with cases like these. The importance of this relation to Beauvoir's ethical thought can also be seen in her analysis of interactions with children. We are constantly constraining the concrete freedom of children, she notes, but we do so with the goal, first, of insuring that they *have* a future and, secondly, of opening up a future rich with possibilities. She says: "To treat him as a child is not to bar him from the future but to open it to him" (EA 141). This rationale does not justify too great a severity, though: the child is a developing freedom who must be consulted about its needs. A child's future stretches out farther into the distance than an adult's and the child's connection with the future gives its needs a certain moral priority. Beauvoir says that the wishes of a couple who persist in living in unhealthy conditions should be honored, except if they have children: "the freedom of the parents would be the ruin of their sons, and as freedom and the future are on the side of the latter, these are the ones who must first be taken into account" (EA 143–144).

Beauvoir emphasizes that intervening in other people's lives like this is usually only justified if one has a concrete bond with them. As a parent, nurse, friend, she says, I take on a commitment to others that can justify using the harsh measures against them that are sometimes necessary to help them. And indeed, barring cases of evident danger or other obvious hazard, an individual usually does not feel free to do the same things to other people's children as one would do to one's own. If as Beauvoir says, "love authorizes severities which are not granted to indifference" (EA 137), it is because I do not have

concrete responsibilities to humanity as a whole. I have them rather
to those persons with whom I am engaged in the actual everyday historically conditioned relations I have committed myself to.

In her discussion of these cases, Beauvoir speaks, as Sartre does in
"Existentialism is a Humanism," of inventing a solution. But she sup-
plies her readers with a guiding idea to steer this invention process:
"To put it positively, the precept will be to treat the other . . . as a freedom so that his end may be freedom; in using this conducting wire
one will have to incur the risk, in each case, of inventing an original
solution" (EA 142). To enable a person to take freedom as his or her
end is to promote that person's moral freedom. This new existentialist conception of freedom that Beauvoir comes up with allows her to
give a content to existentialist ethics that was only barely hinted at in
Sartre's treatment of the topic.

6

Beauvoir's Ethics as an Ethics of Political Liberation

In her essay "Idéalisme morale et réalisme politique," published a few months before she began *The Ethics of Ambiguity*, Beauvoir speaks of an authentic morality for the first time. Notably it is in the context of a discussion about the right attitude to take towards politics. The man who subscribes to traditional morality, which appeals to Kantian principles and Platonic ideals, refuses to compromise his idealism by engaging in the give-and-take of politics, she says. Those who consider themselves political realists, on the other hand, scoff at the constraints of morality, arguing that the end justifies the means. In an authentic morality, by comparison, politics and morality are "confounded" (IMRP 81). Following out this conviction, throughout *The Ethics of Ambiguity*, particularly in the last section, "The Positive Aspect of Ambiguity," Beauvoir discusses morality in a political context. In the previous chapter I discussed Beauvoir's treatment of difficult decisions people are called on to make in the personal sphere. But for her the political arena is the place where moral dilemmas are the most acute.

Yet, notably, Beauvoir does not discuss political theory here. Political theory asks questions about the legitimacy and authority of the state. Perhaps Beauvoir, as someone who recently witnessed the rise of the Nazis to state power in Germany and the institution of the collaborationist Vichy government in France, is disinclined to take the idea of the legitimacy of the state at face value. But Beauvoir states another reason for dismissing political theory: "Politics always puts forward Ideas: Nation, Empire, Union, Economy, etc. But none of these forms has value in itself; it has it only insofar as it involves concrete individuals" (EA 145). To do political theory one must adopt a standpoint that transcends the actual political situation in order to ask highly abstract and hypothetical questions. Political theorists in the past made use of concepts such as the state of nature. John Rawls today talks about something he calls the original position. No one pretends such things ever did or could exist. These abstract standpoints are ones that no real living subject can actually occupy.

Beauvoir's concern with politics is understandable, given the historical times in which she lived. But the way that she expands ethics to include issues of political morality has a philosophical rationale as well, a rationale drawn from the central phenomenological concept of the situated subject. The phenomenological and existentialist tradition holds that a human subject always finds itself 'in situation', that is, in a highly particularized complex of circumstances. A key aspect of one's situation to Beauvoir, as it would be to any European living in the 1940s, is the type of political arrangements one lives under, as well as the general political climate of the time. It is this aspect of politics—the actual present-day political situation that each human confronts—that Beauvoir is concerned with in *The Ethics of Ambiguity*, not political theory. It is this aspect of politics that is relevant to her ethics. For if a human subject is always a subject in situation, then all ethics necessarily involves some sort of political commitment. Each person's situation has a political dimension, so the ethical person cannot escape taking a political position of some kind.

Beauvoir's underlying assumption in *The Ethics of Ambiguity* that an ethical stance involves a political commitment is reminiscent of Sartre's ideal of the engaged intellectual who, he argues in pieces he wrote during this same period, can and should take a political stand through his or her work.[1] In championing this ideal Sartre no doubt was responding to the same historical circumstances that influenced Beauvoir. But I want to argue that this general idea that one's political commitments make up a part of one's ethical stance toward the world and are something for which one can be held accountable is also held by many today. For instance, imagine the case of a white supremacist who, aside from holding these repugnant political views, leads a spotlessly moral life. Most people would still hold him morally culpable for his political views. (A person of African descent who encountered this person might have grounds to judge that he had personal moral failings as well.) This example underlines Beauvoir's point that: "political choice is an ethical choice" (EA 148).

Yet, although many might agree with Beauvoir on this point, some might disagree with her on much else. For which political choice is the ethical one to make? Notice how by using the example of the white supremacist I have stacked the deck. I am assuming that anyone reading this book would reject the doctrine of white supremacy out of hand. But this is not the case for many other doctrines that I might name in its place. Whether or not a person would reject these doctrines and morally condemn those holding them would depend on the political positions he or she happened to hold. Generally speaking, those on the Right decry the morals of those on the Left, while those on the Left condemn the morals of those on the Right. Thus to accept the general principle that one is morally accountable for one's political commitments takes one only so far. The question remains: what political stance or stances is it moral for someone to support, reject, or condemn?

A Moral Commitment to Liberation

Beauvoir herself gives an unequivocal answer to this question. She firmly identified herself with the Left at this point in her intellectual career and remained committed to various radical political causes up until her death. Furthermore, *The Ethics of Ambiguity* contains an argument that provides the moral justification, if not for the particular causes that Beauvoir supported, then for her general commitment to the liberation of the oppressed. Thus Beauvoir does not just assume that to live ethically involves taking a political stand. She argues that we are morally obligated to take a particular political stand, one against oppression and in favor of liberation.

I have sketched out the individual steps of this argument in chapter 4. Briefly put, the argument is that in order to realize the full dimension of one's own freedom—that is, to attain moral freedom—one must be able and willing to interact with other morally free individuals. If one is oneself oppressed one is kept from developing one's own freedom. Once one grasps one's own oppression, then the political stand one is morally obligated to take is resistance, rebellion, or revolt: "the oppressed can fulfill his freedom as a man only in revolt" (EA 87). Beauvoir thus goes beyond political theorists like John Locke who argue that political revolution can be morally justified. For her in certain cases it is morally required. Second, if one is not oneself oppressed one is morally obligated to support the liberation struggles of those who are. When others are oppressed, one is cut off from free interaction with them, and thus one's own freedom is limited. To achieve moral freedom oneself, one must respect, defend, and nurture the moral freedom of others.

In principle at least this stance does not commit one to a struggle without end. This obligation to fight against oppression is not a freestanding tenet of Beauvoir's ethics. Rather it is called into being by the particular historical situations people find themselves in. Beauvoir says:

> Perhaps it is permissible to dream of a future when men will know no other use of their freedom than this free unfurling of itself; constructive activity would be possible for all; each one would be able to aim positively through his projects at his own future. But today the fact is that there are men who can justify their life only by negative action. (EA 81)[2]

At the time that Beauvoir wrote *The Ethics of Ambiguity* she did not see herself as oppressed, even though she was already aware that women tend to be oppressed as a group. Perhaps she saw herself as one of those women who "had in their work an apprenticeship of freedom" (EA 37) and thus had escaped oppression. It was not until she started the project that would become *The Second Sex* right after she finished *The Ethics of Ambiguity* that she realized that the central defining factor in her life was that she was a woman. This was one aspect of her own situation that she had been blind to. Once she realized this bond she had to all other women, she followed the trajectory she laid out in *The Ethics of Ambiguity*. She fought against women's oppression, first by writing *The Second Sex*, and then later by joining with other women to fight for specific feminist causes.

Perhaps because Beauvoir does not see herself to be oppressed, she makes it a priority to argue that a person has an obligation to support the liberation struggles of others. The reason one should fight for the liberation of others can even be seen to be a self-serving one: "If I want the slave to become conscious of his servitude, it is . . . in order that new possibilities might be opened to the liberated slave and through him to all men" (EA 86). The more others are able to develop their freedom, the more I am able to develop mine, according to Beauvoir's central thesis. Yet Beauvoir defers the question of "whether men have to give up the positive use of their freedom as long as the liberation of all has not yet been achieved" (EA 88). Each individual must craft his or her own solution to this dilemma. She says only that, although an outsider cannot be engaged in this struggle to the same extent the oppressed themselves are, "he cannot fulfill himself morally" (EA 89) without taking some part in it.

Defining Oppression

So according to Beauvoir we have a moral obligation to try to overcome our own oppression and the oppression of others. But how do we know who is oppressed? Beauvoir implies in places that the criterion we ultimately must fall back on in deciding whether someone is oppressed is the person's own judgment on the matter. She warns against taking on the attitude of an "enlightened elite" who decide for others that they should be freed from the burden of backwardness (EA 138). Oppression does not exist when one's freedom "has no other limits than those which the subject assigns himself" (EA 83).

However, this criterion of oppression, though certainly consistent with Beauvoir's overall rejection of paternalism, turns out to be less satisfactory than it first appears. For one, it rules out the possibility that people can be oppressed even though they think they are not. And in doing so it raises problems for an analysis of women's oppression. Until fairly recently most women did not consider themselves to be oppressed, while some women even hotly insisted the opposite and continue to do so today. Beauvoir does not want to blame the oppressed for their own oppression. But she sometimes does seem to be hard on women in particular. Critics have charged that even in *The Second Sex* Beauvoir makes it sound too much as if women have colluded in their own oppression.[3] In *The Ethics of Ambiguity* Beauvoir seems to take just this position when she comments that the Western woman of today, if she does not resist her lot, "chooses it or at least consents to it" (EA 38). But if a woman consents to her lot, does that mean that she is *not* oppressed?

Beauvoir makes this comment in distinguishing the case of the Western woman of today from that of the African or harem slave of the past.[4] There exists a "possibility of liberation" for the Western woman, but there did not for these others. The difference lies in the knowledge about their situation available to each. The slave is subject to what Beauvoir calls "mystification": he or she sees his or her condition to be imposed by nature or by the gods. In this case, "it is necessary to bring the seed of his liberation to him from the outside: his submission is not enough to justify the tyranny which is imposed upon him" (EA 85). But in this statement, notice that the slave's assessment of his own position is not the ultimate criterion of whether he is oppressed or not. Thus Beauvoir does not accept the person's own judgment as the criterion of oppression in this case.

The strategy of appealing to the person's own judgment of whether she is oppressed or not runs into another problem, a problem which has become acute recently, but which Beauvoir herself foresaw when she wrote *The Ethics of Ambiguity*. When the privileges of some are taken away in the course of liberating others, it is not at all uncommon for them to complain that they themselves are being oppressed. I remember reading in the newspaper, for instance, about one of Haiti's ruling elite complaining that the advent of democracy had made it impossible for him to drive his Mercedes in the streets of Port-au-Prince any more. More broadly, the rise of feminism and the implementation of affirmative action has led some white males in the United States to claim the status of victims. Beauvoir's concept of moral freedom allows her to distinguish sharply between what she calls the "freedom of exploiting" (EA 90) and true freedom, as I will explore later. But cases like these do give additional reasons to reject the suggestion that a person's own assessment should be the ultimate criterion of oppression.

What appears to be needed in such cases is some objective criterion of oppression, objective not in the sense of capturing the 'real' facts of the situation, which appeals to a false objectivity that Beauvoir ascribes to the spirit of seriousness,[5] but objective in the sense that it is independent of the person's own viewpoint. Beauvoir in fact does offer a characterization of oppression that might be able to generate a standard that one can apply from the outside like this. A person is oppressed, she states, when he is cut off from having a future, for it is the future that, as I explored in chapter 4, gives meaning to his present existence. As Beauvoir puts it, others open the future for me. Instead of opening it, then, they can close it off, denying me the realization of my uniquely human qualities. She says that oppression creates a class of

> those who are condemned to mark time hopelessly in order merely to support the collectivity; their life is a pure repetition of mechanical gestures; their leisure is just about sufficient for them to regain their strength; the oppressor feeds himself on their transcendence and refuses to extend it by a free recognition. (EA 83)

This passage is noteworthy because it extends her definition of oppression to encompass economic as well as political oppression, a point to which I will return later.

Beauvoir's claim that a defining feature of oppression is being cut off from the future suggests that what the oppressed are denied is the ability to attain moral freedom, for what is attained in moral freedom is a truly vital connection to the future. This suggestion, though not explicitly expressed by Beauvoir, provides a rationale for why oppression is morally wrong. According to Beauvoir I can develop my moral freedom only by acting in concert with other morally free agents; thus I have a moral obligation to promote, not to suppress, the moral freedom of others. It also fits into the conventional way of thinking about oppression, according to which what has been taken from the oppressed is precisely their freedom. This conventional understanding that oppression involves the denial of freedom is violated by Sartre's insistence in *Being and Nothingness* that "the slave in chains is as free as his master" (BN 550). Beauvoir's distinction between moral freedom and ontological freedom allows one both to accept a Sartrean position on freedom and to salvage the common-sense view that freedom is something that can be taken away. We always retain ontological freedom whatever circumstances we find ourselves in. What we can be denied by our situation—by other people's control of our situation—is the ability to develop moral freedom.

The Moral Status of the Oppressed

To hold that what the oppressed are denied is the ability to develop moral freedom, however, leads to another problem. Indeed to push this idea to its full extent reveals potential inconsistencies in

Beauvoir's treatment of oppression. The difficulty arises in assigning a moral status to the oppressed. Freedom fighters who work with others to overcome their own oppression achieve the pinnacle of moral freedom according to her view. But the oppressed who do not contest their oppression are left only in possession of their ontological freedom according to the line of thought I have been pursuing: they are not able to realize their moral freedom because they are cut off from creating their own future by their oppressors. But Beauvoir's ethics hinges on the connection she makes between morality and freedom. The essential connection between the two is suggested in the very term "moral freedom." If the oppressed lack moral freedom, the implication is that they somehow are not fully moral.

To suggest that the oppressed are somehow less moral than those who are free is quite shocking. First, what right have we to judge morally those who live under terrible conditions that they have in no way brought upon themselves. Second, it is questionable whether such a characterization is accurate. Some think the opposite—that the downtrodden are more virtuous than the well-off. Beauvoir comes back to this question of the moral status of the oppressed in a number of places, which suggests that it was a sticky issue for her ethics to resolve.

Generally her strategy is to deny that an oppressed person is necessarily less moral or even less free than someone who is not oppressed. She says of the slave: "in his relationships with his friends, for example, he can live as a free and moral man within this world where his ignorance has enclosed him" (EA 85). Yet in insisting that slaves are in no way to blame for the condition they continue to remain in, Beauvoir says that slaves, and to a certain extent women, are like children in that they are forced to live in what she calls the universe of the serious: they do not have the means at their disposal to question the values that this universe comes furnished with. It is contradictory for Beauvoir to compare the situation of slaves to that of children and in the same paragraph to claim that slaves may realize "a perfect assertion of their freedom" (EA 38). Can children realize a perfect assertion of their freedom? In other places she argues that children are the only people whose freedom can justifiedly be limited.[6]

There are other problems that arise from Beauvoir's repeated assertions that freedom is possible even in oppression. For one

thing, if a person can achieve freedom in oppression what motiva-
tion would he or she have to overcome it? Furthermore, if the slave
can realize freedom in slavery, why is what the slave master does
morally wrong? What, if anything, has the slave been deprived of
through his enslavement?

I have already suggested a simple answer to the last question: the
slave is deprived of his ability to develop moral freedom. Beauvoir
does not take this tack in her treatment of oppression, perhaps
because she did not want to give the appearance of condemning those
unfortunate enough to live under such terrible conditions. But by
refusing to take this step Beauvoir fails to pinpoint what diminishment
the oppressed person suffers. Her theory of freedom comes up short
in this regard.

Before I explore another avenue that I think is open to Beauvoir
to take in theorizing oppression, I want to say a little about the moral
status of the oppressed. As I said earlier, some people hold that those
who have been victimized enjoy a higher moral status than do those
who have not. The roots of this assumption lie in a type of faulty
moral arithmetic that people fall into. When someone victimizes
another, he becomes less moral himself, but the moral credit that he
thereby loses does not then accrue to his victim. You are not made a
better person by being subjected to abuse or other forms of oppression; in some ways you are made worse and therein lies the oppressor's moral culpability. This idea that oppression consists in being
deprived of the ability to realize moral freedom might be used to
explain exactly how you are made worse. For when you are oppressed
you are robbed of many possibilities for action that you might otherwise have if you were not oppressed.

However, while being oppressed does not confer a higher moral
status on someone, neither does it automatically make someone a
morally worse person. The oppressed person's moral status, *qua*
oppressed person, is a neutral one. Whereas she does not gain the
moral credit lost by the oppressor, she does not lose moral standing
through being oppressed either, as the strategy of "blaming the victim" makes it seem. One who is actively kept from developing her
freedom does not have much to be blamed for. Only when that person has the choice to embrace moral freedom or to evade it through
the different strategies Beauvoir lays out in the second section of the
book does she have responsibility for that choice. Although one might

expect that someone who has been oppressed herself might be more loathe to oppress others herself, nothing *guarantees* that an oppressed person when presented with the possibility of developing her freedom will act morally. While the oppressed person's moral status *qua* oppressed is neutral, the actual behavior of oppressed people—even under conditions of extreme oppression—can be expected to vary widely, morally speaking, as would the behavior of any group of people. All people, whether oppressed or not, are capable of good or evil, as Beauvoir herself realizes: "certainly the proletarian is no more naturally a moral man than another" (EA 87).

Power and Freedom

How might Beauvoir's theory of freedom be able to explain oppression? In *The Ethics of Ambiguity* Beauvoir makes a few suggestive remarks about the difference between power and freedom, a distinction she previously made in *Pyrrhus et Cinéas*. The way out of the impasse I have described above is to be found in this distinction, I think. In *The Ethics of Ambiguity* she says: "the freedom of man is infinite, but his power is limited" (EA 28).7 The question that I say remains unanswered by Beauvoir's theory is: what exactly is it that is taken away from one in situations of oppression? Beauvoir appears to deny that a person is completely deprived of the ability to realize one's freedom. But what then is taken away? If someone's freedom is infinite, but his or her power can be limited, then perhaps it is a person's power that is curtailed by oppression.

A person's power is limited by many factors, chief among them what existentialists call facticity, which includes both one's material and historical circumstances. As Beauvoir says in the opening passages of *The Ethics of Ambiguity*, a human can be crushed by the "dark weight" of things. In addition, one can choose to limit one's own power, for instance, by respecting another's freedom. I take this to be what Beauvoir means when she says: "it is not true that the recognition of the freedom of others limits my own freedom: to be free is not to have the power to do anything you like" (EA 91). Ontological freedom cannot be limited by anything—this is the Sartrean thesis. And to recognize the moral freedom of others increases rather than limits my moral freedom. But to realize moral freedom by joining together

with others in a common project does limit one's power (for example,
over one's time and material resources). Under conditions of oppression, by contrast, one's power is limited not by oneself but by something else, not a force of nature, but rather another person or persons,
or an institution representing those persons.

Pursuing the question of what exactly the oppressed person can be
said to be deprived of if not her freedom, according to Beauvoir's theory, I have suggested that a good answer is that she is deprived of
power. But this idea, promising though it is, raises still other questions. For instance, what exactly does a person suffer from being
deprived of power in this way and why is doing this to another person
morally wrong? In order to answer these questions it is necessary to
return to the subject of freedom and ask what possible connection
there might be between power and freedom, what Beauvoir calls
moral freedom specifically.

It is wrong to oppress others, according to Beauvoir's argument,
because to be free ourselves—to achieve moral freedom—we need to
extend and not suppress the moral freedom of others. Oppressing
others limits their power, I have speculated. If it is wrong to do this,
it must be because power serves as a foundation, in some way, for the
development of moral freedom. To suggest that power somehow
underpins the development of moral freedom is to suggest that there
is a material basis for moral freedom, for whatever power might turn
out to be, it must involve some sort of interaction with the material
world.

Granted, Beauvoir nowhere says that what she calls power serves
as a condition for the development of moral freedom. But she condemns the Stoic philosophers' "abstract notion of freedom" (EA
29), which subsists even in the face of a severe limitation of power.
She also asserts that "freedom realizes itself only by engaging itself
in the world" (EA 78). Interaction with the material world gives a
content to freedom. The implication is that genuine, moral freedom
is expressed through material means. The full realization of human
freedom cannot take place in isolation from others according to
Beauvoir's argument. Neither can it take place in disengagement
from the material world. A central element of the fundamental
ambiguity that characterizes human existence is the fact that a
human is at the same time a consciousness and a material presence
in the world. The development of moral freedom, like all aspects of

human life, must play itself out against the backdrop of this fundamental ambiguity. A human being always needs a material foundation for its existence.

Of course, a human must have certain material needs fulfilled just to survive. But, as Beauvoir points out, a distinctively human existence requires something over and above the continued existence as a material thing in the world: "Life is occupied in both perpetuating itself and in surpassing itself; if all it does is maintain itself, then living is only not dying, and human existence is indistinguishable from an absurd vegetation" (EA 83). For this reason, Beauvoir goes on to argue that "those who are condemned to mark time hopelessly in order merely to support the collectivity," whose life is "a pure repetition of mechanical gestures" (EA 82–83), without leisure, are oppressed. They are kept from realizing their full dimension as human beings. This definition of oppression Beauvoir offers, as I remarked earlier, focuses more on economic oppression than political oppression. But she does note elsewhere how the strategy of making people's lives meaningless by making them perform meaningless tasks, for instance, emptying and filling a ditch, is a favored technique of political oppression.[8]

That oppression can and often does take on an economic form according to Beauvoir shows that there must be some sort of material basis for moral freedom, at least on the assumption that oppression involves the denial of moral freedom. A further consequence of this idea is that the ethical person has an obligation to try to combat economic oppression. If a certain level of material well-being is required in order for humans to realize moral freedom, then the person seeking moral freedom herself has an obligation to help supply them with this minimal level of material well-being, since for her to realize her moral freedom others must realize theirs as well. Beauvoir does not discuss this aspect of moral commitment in *The Ethics of Ambiguity*, but she does allude to it in *Pyrrhus et Cinéas*, where she says, "I demand for men health, knowledge, well-being, leisure in order that their freedom does not consume itself in fighting sickness, ignorance and misery" (PC 115). She nowhere discusses the possible role that the state might play in promoting people's freedom in any of her ethical essays. However, the idea that moral freedom requires a material foundation provides a reason for the state to guarantee a certain basic level of material well-being to all. This is a socialist conception of the role of the state, of course.[9] Although disappointed by actual socialist governments, Beauvoir declared later in life: "I have always believed that socialism was a more enlightened form of government than the so-called liberalism of earlier French governments."[10]

My conclusions here are tentative. For one thing, Beauvoir does not give much indication of what she means when she uses the term power. I have interpreted the term in a somewhat materialistic vein to mean humans' ability to engage in the material world, to interact with it to fulfill their material needs and to launch their projects. (Two examples Beauvoir gives in *Pyrrhus et Cinéas* of *restraining* someone's power are throwing him into prison and cutting off his arms.[11] To accept this interpretation of what power is and my further hypothesis that power serves in some way as the material basis of moral freedom is to see Beauvoir as more of a materialist than she herself later judged she was at this point in her development. In *Force of Circumstance* she reproached herself: "Why did I write *concrete liberty* instead of *bread*?"[12] If what I am saying about there being a material basis to moral freedom is right, then bread, and the material conditions of life generally, are a concern of Beauvoir's ethics.

On the other hand, to take an ethics of liberation too far in a materialistic direction has its pitfalls too, notwithstanding Beauvoir's advocacy of a materialist approach in *Force of Circumstance*. For there certainly are people who lead a life of relative abundance who are still oppressed. The dutiful bourgeois daughters, wives, and mothers whose lives Beauvoir depicts in *The Second Sex* are a good case in point. In this work Beauvoir posits what is basically a psychological mechanism—the making of a group of people into the Other—as the basis of women's oppression. In her treatment of the female body in this work Beauvoir suggests that there is a material basis to women's oppression as well, but these sections of *The Second Sex* remain controversial to this day.[13]

Yet the body is not merely a material entity. Indeed the human body provides a good example of how the distinction between a materialist and an idealist ethics that Beauvoir makes in her remarks in *Force of Circumstance* is based on a false dichotomy. The body is part of the material basis of human life, and controlling the body is a way to oppress people, but the body is also an extension of consciousness. This central thesis of Merleau-Ponty's *Phenomenology of Perception* was one that Beauvoir endorsed and incorporated into *The Second Sex*.[14] The same insight lies at the basis of Beauvoir's concept of human ambiguity. Human life is a totality. It cannot be reduced to either a purely material or a purely mental existence. An existentialist ethics must reflect this fundamental ambiguity. Since human existence spans these two categories, then, an existentialist ethics must speak to both the material and nonmaterial aspects of human life. It can be neither an idealist nor a materialist ethics.

Fighting Oppression

I have tried to show that Beauvoir's theory of freedom can be extended by further developing her concept of power in order to generate a more complete description of what oppression consists in. Oppression, I hypothesize, involves denying one the ability to develop moral freedom by creating a future of one's own in joint projects with others. One way it can be brought about is through curtailing a person's power, or ability to interact with the material world. To free others from oppression, then, requires insuring that they have at least a minimal level of material well-being. (In philosophical terms, this minimal level of well-being is a necessary but not a sufficient condition of moral freedom.) And, I reiterate, according to Beauvoir's central thesis in *The Ethics of Ambiguity* we have a moral obligation to attempt to overcome oppression.

But *how* should one set about overcoming oppression? Beauvoir has quite a bit to say on this topic. First, there are certain limits that should be respected when dealing with those who are not aware of their own oppression. In the case of the slave who has been subjected to mystification and thus is wholly ignorant of the roots of his condition, she says, as we have seen: "it is necessary to bring the seed of his liberation to him from the outside" (EA 85). She is not specific about what might serve as a seed of liberation in such cases, but presumably education would be of central importance, or anything that combats mystification and thus puts the oppressed "in the presence of his freedom" (EA 87). This is what Beauvoir herself can be said to have done for women as a whole by writing *The Second Sex*. The testimony of many women that reading this book changed their lives shows the extent to which women, even well-educated Western women, have also been the victims of mystification and not the complicitous dupes that she suggests at one point in *The Ethics of Ambiguity.*

But once the slave has been put in the presence of his freedom, Beauvoir says, then the next step is up to him. It is wrong to attempt, in Rousseau's words, to "force him to be free."[15] For one, it is foolish because, due to their ontological freedom, no one ultimately can force other human beings to do anything, least of all freely embrace freedom. As Beauvoir insists in *Pyrrhus et Cinéas*, we can do nothing for others except create a point of departure for them. Secondly, forcing liberation on people against their will can have unforeseen and unfortunate consequences: "Certainly it is not a question of throwing men in spite of themselves, under the pretext of liberation, into a new world, one which they have not chosen, on which they have no grip . . . these false liberations . . . overwhelm those who are their victims as if they were a new blow of blind fate" (EA 85–86).[16] In liberating people one has a responsibility to concern oneself with what happens to them after the moment of liberation. Beauvoir feels that we should appeal to people's own experience of their situation in dealing with oppression. Whereas we sometimes cannot depend on people's own judgment as to whether they are oppressed or not, we should respect their judgment as to whether they should be liberated or not. Beauvoir's position that no one can bring another "salvation from the outside" (EA 106) is certainly consistent with existentialist notions of freedom.

A Justification for Political Violence

One thing that distinguishes political morality from personal morality is that questions about whether the use of force is justified usually only arise in the political sphere. Beauvoir's ethics is noteworthy in that she offers a conditional defense of the use of political violence. The cases in which the use of physical violence is morally justified are those where it is used as a last resort against an oppressor in order to overcome oppression. However, the argument that Beauvoir gives for the use of force in these cases is quite dense and, when unpacked, somewhat unconvincing.

First, there is the issue of the status of the oppressor's freedom. As I mentioned earlier, when a ruling elite is being overthrown they often complain that their freedom is being suppressed. But according to Beauvoir's point of view, the oppressor in oppressing others is failing to realize his moral freedom. He makes only a negative use of his freedom by utilizing the power at his disposal and thus by his own choice remains at the level of ontological freedom. For this reason the morally free person has no obligation to defend the freedom of the oppressor. On the contrary, she has an obligation to promote the development of the freedom of the oppressed, which is blocked by the oppressor. If the realization of the oppressed's moral freedom conflicts with the oppressor's exercise of his ontological freedom, it is even permissible to attempt to curtail his exercise of it. Beauvoir says: "We have to respect freedom only when it is intended for freedom, not when it strays, flees itself, and resigns itself. A freedom which is interested only in denying freedom must be denied" (EA 90–91).

The only way to curtail the exercise of the oppressor's freedom in certain cases is through physical violence. Beauvoir's argument that violence is morally justified in these cases begins by considering the way that the ontological freedom of the oppressor is experienced by those he oppresses. In moral freedom one person's freedom is intertwined with another's. But since he isolates himself from the human community, the oppressor's freedom is experienced by the oppressed as a blind force of nature acting on them from the outside: "by virtue of the fact that the oppressors refuse to cooperate in the affirmation of freedom, they embody, in the eyes of all men of good will, the absurdity of facticity" (EA 97). Facticity, once again, is the existentialist term for that aspect of my situation that is pre-given and contingent. Moral freedom, by actively disclosing the world—making being be—is a "triumph of freedom over facticity" (EA 97). Thus it is consistent with moral freedom that the oppressor's ontological freedom, which is experienced as a blind force of nature, be triumphed over.

But how can the freedom of the oppressor be overcome? One cannot suppress the ontological freedom of others, for they always retain this level of freedom whatever the circumstances. Since the ontological freedom of the oppressor is out of reach, one must act on the "objective presence" of his body: "since their subjectivity, by definition, escapes our control, it will be possible to act only on their objective presence; others will here have to be treated like things, with violence" (EA 97). Because the oppressor's freedom is experienced by the oppressed as a blind force of nature that must be overcome, physical force used against the material presence of his body can be morally justified.

I see at least two shortcomings to this argument. First, Beauvoir does not explore how targeting the oppressor's power, not his freedom, might be sufficient to overcome oppression. After all, what effect does acting on the material presence of others have on their freedom? Of course, death puts an end to human freedom.[17] But imprisoning someone is an act of physical violence too. In this case I hypothesize that violence works by limiting a person's power, for power can be limited "from the outside" (PC 86), unlike freedom. Short of killing a person there is no way one can actually negate another's freedom using material means, as the Stoic philosophers emphasized. Limiting a person's power by putting him in prison does allow one to limit the exercise of this person's ontological freedom. And that may be all that is needed. For the most significant effect the exercise of the oppressor's ontological freedom has is to deny those he oppresses the ability to develop their moral freedom. So violence of this type against the oppressor might be justified because it prevents further acts of oppression. Beauvoir appeals to this type of utilitarian argument in her memoirs to justify the execution of war criminals after the war.[18] However, she does not take this tack in *The Ethics of Ambiguity*.

Another problem with this argument is that it does not identify the most salient feature of the relation between the oppressor and the oppressed, morally speaking. The justification for using violence against the oppressor cannot be merely that the oppressor in refusing moral freedom reverts to the level of facticity and thus invites retaliation. Elsewhere she argues that a person can never sink back to the level of facticity. In any case, humans are never oppressed by things, only by other humans: "one does not submit to a war or an occupation as he does to an earthquake" (EA 82). Nature is not responsible for the injuries it causes human beings. Humans, on the other hand, are responsible for the injuries they cause other humans. Even if those who are severely oppressed come to look on their condition as somehow imposed by fate and their oppressors as impersonal agents of their misfortune, their oppressors are still responsible for what they have done. When Beauvoir describes how the actions of the oppressor are experienced as a blind force of nature, she glosses over this fact. It is the responsibility that the oppressor bears for his actions that would seem to justify him suffering in return for the suffering he has inflicted. Unlike a force of nature, the oppressor is morally accountable for what he does.

This observation harks back to the argument Beauvoir gives in her essay "Oeil pour oeil" for why the execution of Nazi war criminals and their French collaborators was justified. In such cases, she argues, violent revenge answers a deep metaphysical need to redress the imbalance that these people's own use of violence has created. In *The Ethics of Ambiguity* Beauvoir describes the relation between the oppressor and the oppressed in the same terms as she describes the relation between the torturer and his victim in "Oeil pour oeil": "of the ambiguous condition which is that of all men, he retains for himself only the aspect of a transcendence which is capable of justifying itself; for the others, the contingent and unjustified aspect of immanence" (EA 102). Beauvoir might have been better off using an argument like the argument she uses in "Oeil pour oeil" to show that using physical violence against the oppressor is sometimes morally justified, rather than the one that she offers in *The Ethics of Ambiguity*.

In the end, Beauvoir seems a bit too sanguine about the necessity for political violence. She does cringe somewhat at the spectacle of the oppressed themselves "become masters, tyrants and executioners" (EA 97). But she feels that one must countenance political violence if one refuses to countenance oppression. She even goes so far as to declare: "A freedom which is occupied in denying freedom is itself so outrageous that the outrageousness of the violence which one practices against it is almost canceled out" (EA 97). In chapter 5 I discussed how one can never be absolutely sure whether an action is morally right according to existentialist ethics. Why would this not be true in the area of political morality as well? Violence may be justified in some political circumstances, say Hitler's Germany or even occupied France, but it seems wrong to claim that its vicious element can be simply "canceled out." There is an undeniable Hegelian flavor to this passage and to the passages in the closing pages of the book where Beauvoir endorses the necessity of "crime and tyranny" and of a "dialectic which goes from freedom to freedom through dictatorship and oppression" (EA 155). Elsewhere in *The Ethics of Ambiguity* Beauvoir charges that Hegel's term "aufheben" can be stretched to encompass both the acceptance and the rejection of a given state of affairs, which leads to "an optimism which denies failure and death" (EA 84). Beauvoir can be accused of promoting a similar optimism with regard to political violence.

Other important moral issues are raised by political violence. Often the oppressor is not the only victim of this violence; usually many innocent people suffer as well. In particular, those who fight oppression through violent means risk losing their own lives or being imprisoned, tortured, and so forth. These people's suffering cannot be canceled out, she says, by any appeal to the cause of the "liberation of man" or similar ideologies. Each individual has a relation, not to the collectivity, but to other individuals. Being irreplaceable, each person has "a unique and irreducible value" (EA 107).

By contrast, one of the strategies of political oppression is to degrade the value of the individual to the point that sacrifice, indeed the loss of life generally, does become meaningless. They do this by reducing humans to their mere material presence, to facticity, to flesh:

> Reduced to pure facticity, congealed in his immanence, cut off from his future, deprived of his transcendence and of the world that transcendence discloses, a man no longer appears as anything more than a thing among things which can be subtracted from the collectivity of other things without its leaving upon the earth any trace of its absence. Multiply this paltry existence by thousands of copies and its insignificance remains; mathematics also teaches us that zero multiplied by any finite number remains zero." (EA 100)

For those fighting oppression to devalue loss and sacrifice by appeal to a collectivist conception of humanity is to lean towards the viewpoint of those they are fighting against.

Hard Choices

According to Beauvoir's ethics, in order to realize moral freedom a person must work to realize the moral freedom of others. This involves, in certain contexts, at least, a commitment to the liberation of the oppressed. In extreme circumstances, Beauvoir sanctions violent resistance or revolution in order to fulfill this commitment. But how can one know whether, when, or how to resort to extreme measures like these? Beauvoir can give no set answer to these questions. Instead she discusses how the moral commitment to fighting against oppression often necessitates making extremely difficult decisions.

If the struggle becomes violent some of those fighting will die and their loved ones will suffer. Some who have nothing to do with the struggle will also suffer. These include those who just happen to be in the wrong place at the wrong time who "die in astonishment, anger or despair" (EA 108). Even without violent struggle, commitment to the political liberation of one group means that one cannot support other valid causes. Situations might even arise where one has to fight against other valid causes.[19] Pursuing liberation for oneself or others requires choosing "between the negation of one freedom or another" (EA 113).

It is the necessity of having to choose between such unpalatable alternatives that drives the moral idealist away from politics. But that does not mean that the political realist is right to declare that morality has nothing to do with politics. An authentic morality does engage itself with politics, Beauvoir says in "Idéalisme morale et réalisme politique." She just does not say how. In *The Ethics of Ambiguity* she struggles to come up with some criteria to appeal to in making difficult decisions like these.

Ultimately Beauvoir offers what she calls a standard of utility to decide what political strategy is justified in particular cases. But what utility consists in for her is not what it consists in for utilitarianism. What is useful, she reasons, is what is useful, not to humanity as a whole, but to a particular group of humans. Furthermore, what is useful now can only be judged in relation to the future, not the static future conceptualized by Enlightenment advocates of progress or messianic religious and political movements, but the "human future" or "living and finite future" (EA 120, 128).

This future is the future sketched out by a particular group of people working together to realize their moral freedom. It is different from the reified future appealed to by the above movements in that it is not separated by a gulf of unrealized moments from the present:

> there is a liberation of man only if, in aiming at itself, freedom is achieved absolutely in the very fact of aiming at itself. This requires that each action be considered as a finished form whose different moments, instead of fleeing toward the future in order to find there their justification, reflect and confirm one another so well that there is no longer a sharp separation between present and future, between means and ends. . . . The liberation aimed at is not a *thing* situated in an unfamiliar time. (EA 130–31)

In liberation struggles the present action, which is an exercise of moral freedom, holds within it the future goal, which is the further realization of moral freedom. Given this goal one cannot predict with much certainty what people will do with their freedom, or potential to realize freedom, once liberated. Indeed we are wrong to have any definite expectations: "insofar as we no longer have a hold on the time which will flow beyond its [liberation's] coming, we must not expect anything of that time for which we have worked" (EA 128).

Beauvoir's method for sorting out the different alternatives the situation we are in presents us with involves "a perpetual contestation of the means by the end and the end by the means" (EA 155). The means must be consistent with the end, not just actually advance it. At the same time we should not evaluate the means in abstraction from the ends they propose to serve. For instance, in regard to Stalinist policies in the U.S.S.R., Beauvoir says: "Suppressing a hundred opponents is surely an outrage, but it may have meaning and a reason; it is a matter of maintaining a regime which brings to an immense mass of men a bettering of their lot" (EA 146). Yet Beauvoir seems perfectly aware that Stalin was guilty of more than suppressing a hundred opponents: "Doubtless, the purges, the deportations, the abuses of the occupation, and the police dictatorship surpass in importance the violence practiced by any other country" (EA 146). On the other hand, those actions that realize values antithetical to moral freedom cannot be justified by the end of defending freedom, as Western democracies that supported dictatorships in order to stop the spread of communism claimed. It is contradictory to deny freedom in order to defend it.

This criterion of utility can validate quite different courses of action in similar circumstances. For example, Beauvoir judges that the labor leader in a Steinbeck novel is right to launch a strike that causes great hardship, whereas the main character in a Dos Passos novel decides rightfully *not* to sacrifice the lives of three miners on trial, although it will advance the cause of the Communist Party.[20]

Furthermore, using this method does not rule out the possibility of error. Beauvoir stresses here as elsewhere how the risk of failure dogs all human undertakings. Not being able to see into the future (since there is nothing there now to see), a person's perspective is always rooted in a particular situation in one point in time. He or she has only an imperfect grasp of all the factors involved. What seemed like the right political position at the time may prove to have been deeply mistaken. Yet often one is forced to choose *now* or the moment for choice slips away. Nonetheless, Beauvoir insists, choice is not thus arbitrary. Beauvoir likens the choice of a political strategy to coming up with a scientific hypothesis. Indeed looking back on the history of science it is easy to find many scientific hypotheses that subsequently have been proven to be wrong. But these failures have done nothing to dent science's reputation for rigor and exactitude.

One might think that the risks involved in political action are greater in situations of violent conflict. Perhaps the pressure to act always seems more intense then. But ironically, as Beauvoir and other French intellectuals learned after the war, political action is much more complicated during peacetime. It is harder to choose between different options because the differences between them are not so stark. So, although the stakes might not seem as high, the risk of failure is even greater. As Beauvoir repeats: "revolt alone is pure" (EA 132).

Especially in situations like this, Beauvoir says, having a political commitment to realizing freedom involves living in "a permanent tension" and subjecting oneself to an "indefinite questioning" (EA 133) of one's motives and assumptions. But living this tension does not erase happiness and joy from one's life. Liberation would be pointless if there were no joy in existence: "If the satisfaction of an old man drinking a glass of wine counts for nothing, then production and wealth are only hollow myths" (EA 135). Freedom assumes its concrete form in pleasure and happiness, she says.

Yet the ultimate consolation for all the difficulties of living a life of moral freedom lies in the fact that one has chosen this life oneself. This choice is an affirmation that human freedom is real. Furthermore, this affirmation involves a distinctive way of living one's freedom. Freedom is no longer a sentence imposed on one from above, as Sartre's assertion that we are condemned to be free suggests. When Beauvoir states that we are absolutely free it means something other than what Sartre means by this. Sartre means that our ontological freedom cannot be limited from the outside. Beauvoir means that through immersion in our projects, through involvement with others, through interaction with the material world, through political commitment we decide ourselves the true extent of our freedom:

> Regardless of the staggering dimensions of the world about us, the density of our ignorance, the risks of catastrophes to come, and our individual weakness within the immense collectivity, the fact remains that we are absolutely free

today if we choose to will our existence in its finiteness, a finiteness that is open on the infinite. (EA 159)

If we will ourselves free by willing others free we can achieve a higher level of freedom, and that, Beauvoir suggests, is its own reward.

7

Connections between *The Ethics of Ambiguity* and *The Second Sex*

I do not intend to present a full-blown analysis of *The Second Sex* here. My focus is *The Ethics of Ambiguity* and the writings leading up to it, because that is where Beauvoir sets out her existentialist ethics. Commentators have already written a great deal on *The Second Sex*. Some, like the four authors I discussed in chapter 1, approach the work from a philosophical perspective. Karen Vintges points out the Sartrean and Hegelian influence on the work and discusses how Beauvoir's roots in the phenomenological movement and her commitment to the concept of the situated subject determined her methodology. Debra Bergoffen adds an emphasis on Beauvoir's alignment with Merleau-Ponty's views on the body. Eva Lundgren-Gothlin discerns the influence of Marxist ideas of history alongside the Hegelian and phenomenological elements in the work. Sonia Kruks also places the book within the phenomenological tradition and sees Beauvoir as taking an original approach to freedom there. (I will discuss her interpretation later.) Many feminist philosophers have closely analyzed the philosophical presuppositions of *The Second Sex* as well.[1] My aim is only to compare the philosophical framework of *The Second Sex* to that of *The Ethics of Ambiguity*. This is a rather modest goal, given the importance of the work, but it generates some significant insights nonetheless. The wording of some passages from *The Second Sex* takes on new meaning in light of my preceding analysis of *The Ethics of Ambiguity*.

Beauvoir initially intended *The Second Sex* to have a close connection to *The Ethics of Ambiguity*. She told her biographer Deirdre Bair that she planned the new essay she started in October 1946 to be a continuation of the work she had just finished, one that expressed her stance towards life as "both woman and existentialist."[2] But by the time she finished the work in June 1949 it had taken on a radically different form than she had originally planned. Obviously its scope grew. The information she includes from the fields of history, biology, anthropology, psychology, and sociology almost obscures its philosophical foundation, especially in the English edition where the translator mistranslates many key philosophical terms.[3] Paying close attention to selected passages in the book, however, can bring this philosophical foundation back into focus.

Themes from *The Ethics of Ambiguity* in *The Second Sex*

There is a particularly important passage in this regard at the end of Beauvoir's introduction. Few seem to have understood its significance, because most of her readers were not aware that Beauvoir herself was the author of an existentialist ethics. The book owed its enormous success to the fact that many of the women who were drawn to read it were not necessarily intellectuals at all. Besides, most intellectuals associated Sartre's name with existentialism, not Beauvoir's. In this passage Beauvoir declares:

> The perspective that we are adopting is that of existentialist ethics. Every subject asserts itself concretely as a transcendence through its projects. It only achieves freedom through a continual reaching out for other freedoms. There is no other justification for its present existence except an expansion towards an indefinite open future. (DS I 31; TSS xxxiv–xxxv)[4]

She touches on several themes central to *The Ethics of Ambiguity* in this passage. The freedom that one achieves by reaching out towards other freedoms and towards an open finite future is what I have called moral freedom. Furthermore, seeking after genuine freedom in this way provides a justification for one's existence, indeed the only real justification of it.

There is another passage later in the book that also summarizes Beauvoir's conclusions in *The Ethics of Ambiguity*:

It is the existence of other men that tears each man out of his immanence and enables him to fulfill the truth of his being, to complete himself through transcendence, through escape toward an objective, through projects. . . . Man attains an authentically moral attitude when he renounces *being* to assume his existence . . . but the conversion by which he attains true wisdom is never complete; it demands a constant tension. (DS I 231-32; TSS 140)

As Beauvoir explains in *The Ethics of Ambiguity*, to renounce being and assume one's existence is not to give in to the desire for being that all humans are haunted by but rather to make oneself into a lack of being in order to actively disclose being. Involvement with other people is the key to this process in this passage, as it is in *The Ethics of Ambiguity*.

In still another passage, Beauvoir applies a conclusion that she comes to in *The Ethics of Ambiguity* to the case of women, the conclusion that "the oppressed can fulfill his freedom . . . only in revolt" (EA 87). In *The Second Sex* she says:

freedom in woman remains abstract and empty, she can authentically assume it only in revolt: that is the only road open to those who have no opportunity of doing anything constructive. They must refuse the limits of their situation and seek to open the road of the future. (DS II 455; TSS 627)

The freedom that is only abstract and empty in women is the freedom that all humans share, ontological freedom. Opening the road to the future is important because, as she says in *The Ethics of Ambiguity*, oppression occurs when someone's future is closed off by others. To seek to open the road of the future is to seek to develop moral freedom. The implication of this passage from *The Second Sex* is that this is what women should seek to do.

The way that these themes from *The Ethics of Ambiguity* are repeated in these passages shows that the perspective that Beauvoir announces she is adopting in *The Second Sex* is that of her own existentialist ethics. Commentators are thus wrong to say that Sartre's *Being and Nothingness* is the philosophical foundation of the work.[5]

Immanence and Transcendence

However, there is a notable shift in focus in *The Second Sex*. Beauvoir does not say a great deal about freedom of any sort there. Instead she relies extensively on the concepts of immanence and transcendence to provide a metaphysical foundation for her analysis of woman's oppression. This distinction between immanence and transcendence cuts across her earlier distinction between ontological and moral freedom and eventually comes to eclipse it. At the same time her reliance on it leads to certain problems.

Beauvoir introduced the concept of transcendence in *Pyrrhus et Cinéas* and uses it also in *The Ethics of Ambiguity* and "Oeil pour oeil." The concept of immanence, which is the opposite of transcendence, is found mainly in *The Second Sex*. In the same passage from the introduction where Beauvoir talks about existentialist ethics, she says: "Every time that transcendence falls back into immanence, there is a degradation of existence into the "in-itself," of freedom into facticity" (DS I 31; TSS xxxv). These terms can be understood in light of Beauvoir's thesis about human ambiguity in *The Ethics of Ambiguity*: humans exist both as material beings and as consciousnesses. Immanence and transcendence are different terms for these two opposing poles. Transcendence is associated with consciousness and purposeful activity. The language she uses sometimes suggests that Beauvoir equates transcendence with freedom, but simply to identify them is problematic, as I will show later. When transcendence "falls back into immanence," on the other hand, a human being becomes engulfed by or identified with the material side of existence. In this quote Beauvoir associates immanence with the Sartrean concepts of facticity and the in-itself.

This opposition between immanence and transcendence is also prefigured in the opposition between subjectivity and material existence that Beauvoir sets up in her essay "Oeil pour oeil." People like the Nazi war criminals commit "an absolute evil" in attempting to reduce their victims to mere things by stripping them of their subjectivity, she says. To do so violates their very humanity, since it denies the ambiguous nature of their existence as both conscious and material beings. Making the victimizer assume the role of the victim in turn makes him realize that he and his former victim share these two dimensions of existence. In *The Second Sex* Beauvoir does not discuss humans' ambiguous existence, but she does say that "every existent is at once immanence and transcendence" (DS I 385; TSS 255).

Beauvoir uses this opposition between immanence and transcendence to explain in philosophical terms how and why women have come to be oppressed by men and male-dominated culture. First, it is important to note that Beauvoir's opinion of the magnitude of women's oppression clearly changed radically after she wrote *The Ethics of Ambiguity*. While she admits there that the woman locked in the harem is obviously oppressed, she seems to feel that Western women can easily escape this fate. Evidently the research and close examination of her life and the lives of other women she engaged in before writing *The Second Sex* convinced her otherwise. Beauvoir added her new insight into the extent of women's oppression to her conviction that oppression is wrong and that everyone has a moral obligation to fight it, the thesis that she argued for in *The Ethics of Ambiguity*. Then she sat down to write *The Second Sex*, which went on to make a major contribution to the cause of women's liberation.

In *The Second Sex* Beauvoir starts from the premise that women share the same human characteristics that men do: "It is regardless of sex that the existent seeks justification through transcendence" (DS I 112; TSS 65). However, women have been assigned an existence as immanence by masculine culture, and have either chosen to accept such an existence or have been forced into it. Beauvoir's suggestion that women have somehow colluded in their own oppression has infuriated some feminist critics.[6] In the introduction Beauvoir traces women's "deep-seated tendencies toward complicity" to humans' inherent desire for being: "the temptation to flee one's freedom and make oneself into a thing" (DS I 21; TSS xxvii). Men, presumably, are not free from these tendencies; but since their social situation is different they are not manifested in the same way. In the conclusion of the book Beauvoir claims, by contrast, that women's condition is not chosen by them but rather imposed on them and consequently strikes a more militant pose: "It is neither an immutable essence or a mistaken choice that has doomed her to immanence, to inferiority. They were imposed on her. All oppression creates a state of war. This case is no exception. The existent that is considered inessential cannot help but demand a reestablishment of its sovereignty." (DS II 561; TSS 717).

The Second Sex describes many ways that women have been cut off from transcendence and consigned to immanence. Beauvoir sees the same basic social phenomenon underlying all of them. Following Hegel, Beauvoir asserts that humans and, more importantly, groups of humans are naturally driven to set up an Other, existing separate from and in opposition to them. Furthermore, the individual or the group defines itself by assigning to this Other all the traits that it does not possess or does not want to possess. Simply put, men as a group have defined themselves as rational, active beings—as transcendence—by differentiating themselves from women, whom they see as remaining mired in immanence. Women are bodies, not minds, close to nature, hostile to culture, and so on. What role biology plays in this process for Beauvoir is a matter of controversy among commentators.[7] But, for whatever reason, women have never contested their identification with immanence. (At least they had not at the time *The Second Sex* was written.) Women do not turn the tables by regarding men as the Other, as other racial groups do, for instance, with regard to whites. Even though woman is defined as immanence, she, like any other human being, exists also as a transcendence. But this fact is covered over in a simple fashion: "whenever she behaves as a human being, she is said to imitate the male" (DS I 98; TSS 51).

Beauvoir shows how and why women themselves come to accept men's definition of them as immanence in the detailed chapters on childhood, sexuality, and social roles in the second volume. To put it in the terms Beauvoir uses in *The Ethics of Ambiguity*, women accept their lot because they are subject to mystification. In *The Ethics of Ambiguity* Beauvoir already saw how mystification is a potent instrument of social control. But only in *The Second Sex* does she comes to grips with how powerful and ubiquitous an instrument it is. The war criminals she writes about in "Oeil pour oeil" use brutal physical force to strip their victims of their subjectivity. Women, for the most part, are denied transcendence through far gentler, but still extremely effective means.

Problems with This Approach

As the preceding shows, the concepts of immanence and transcendence serve fairly well as a philosophical framework for Beauvoir's analysis of women's oppression. But problems arise with this schema if one pursues certain questions far enough. These same questions also reveal certain difficulties in connecting up this schema with Beauvoir's treatment of freedom in *The Ethics of Ambiguity*.

The first question in this regard is how it is possible for a human being to be able to "fall back into immanence." Immanence represents the material side of human existence. But, as Beauvoir asserts in *The Ethics of Ambiguity* and in "Oeil pour oeil," no human being is merely a material existence. That is why it is wrong for any person to treat another human being as if he or she were. In *The Ethics of Ambiguity* Beauvoir states, in agreement with Sartre, that every human possesses an original freedom.[8] This level of freedom is what I have labeled ontological freedom. Saying that a human being can be reduced to immanence, as Beauvoir suggests women have been, implies that a person's ontological freedom can be diminished or taken away. This idea seems to go against a basic tenet of existentialism, which takes human freedom as a given. Sartre, at least, claims that all humans are always free.

Sonia Kruks solves this problem by differentiating Beauvoir's approach to freedom in *The Second Sex* from the position Sartre takes on freedom in *Being and Nothingness*. Yes, Sartre does hold that humans are always free. But according to Kruks Beauvoir gradually came to disagree, even though she continued to claim she was working within a Sartrean framework. Kruks points out that Sartre (at least at the time that he wrote *Being and Nothingness*) would never accept that a conscious human being can, as Beauvoir describes it, fall back into immanence: "Strictly speaking, within Sartre's usage of the terms, the degradation of an existence into the in-itself would have to mean that the oppressed woman has actually ceased to be human."[9] For Beauvoir, Kruks claims, although the woman remains human, her ontological freedom is "reduced to no more than a suppressed potentiality."[10] This potentiality for freedom at least can never be completely erased.

In her interpretation Kruks follows the schema of immanence and transcendence that Beauvoir employs in *The Second Sex* through to its logical conclusion. Since Beauvoir seems to associate freedom with transcendence, its opposite, immanence, would have to involve the loss of freedom. I wonder, though, what the real difference is between what Kruks describes as the potential for freedom, which women do always retain according to her, and what I have been calling ontological freedom. Is not ontological freedom merely the ability to act or the ability to choose, whether or not that ability is ever exercised? Of course, under conditions of severe oppression a person is kept by psychological or physical means from exercising ontological freedom. In that sense it is only a potentiality.

Instead of accepting the idea that freedom can be taken away from a person, I would be inclined to argue that what happens under conditions of oppression, especially internalized oppression, is that people are prevented from becoming aware of their freedom. Subjected to massive mystification, they are unaware of what they are capable of, unaware even of the few opportunities for change they do have. That is why Beauvoir says that the seeds of their liberation must be brought them from the outside. This idea conflicts, of course, with the assumption existentialism makes that people always are aware at some level that they are free. (That is what leads to anguish and drives them to flee their freedom in bad faith.) But I would be more willing to give up this assumption than to give up on the idea that all people are in some sense free.

In my analysis of Beauvoir's treatment of oppression in *The Ethics of Ambiguity* I speculated that what is taken away from a person in this situation is the ability to develop moral freedom. Once one distinguishes between different senses of freedom, to say that under certain conditions a person is both free and unfree does not involve a contradiction. Indeed I have contended that Beauvoir is actually working with three senses of freedom: ontological freedom, power (which is concrete freedom) and moral freedom. The oppressed person, according to my interpretation, retains ontological freedom but is deprived of power and the ability to develop moral freedom. This explanation for what occurs in oppression suggests a possible way to hook up Beauvoir's concepts of ontological and moral freedom in *The Ethics of Ambiguity* with the concepts of immanence and transcendence in *The Second Sex*: immanence can be seen as the bare possession of ontological freedom and transcendence as the exercise of moral freedom. The idea is that the person reduced to immanence through being oppressed still retains ontological freedom but that is the *only* type of freedom this person possesses. Oppression involves a diminishment of power and I have speculated that a person requires a sufficient amount of power in order to develop moral freedom.

Nonetheless, it is not possible to identify moral freedom with transcendence for one important reason. The problem is that Beauvoir associates transcendence with male behavior in *The Second Sex*, and men, as the oppressors, cannot be said to realize moral freedom according to Beauvoir's argument in *The Ethics of Ambiguity*. Through making women into the Other, men have reserved all the activities that are a means to transcendence for themselves. As Eva Lundgren-Gothlin, who also sees Beauvoir's use of the concept of transcendence in relation to male behavior to be problematic, says: "in *The Second Sex* Beauvoir tends to see the situation of all men as transcendence and that of all women as immanent."[11] Beauvoir even suggests that men are driven to set up an Other as an act of transcendence: "Once the subject seeks to assert himself, the Other who limits and denies him, is nonetheless a necessity to him" (DS I 231; TSS 139). Transcendence thus cannot be the same thing as moral freedom, because in order to achieve moral freedom, not only can one not oppress others, one must try to enable others to achieve moral freedom as well.

These reflections point to another problem with Beauvoir's distinction between transcendence and immanence. One thing that it cannot account for is why the oppression of women is morally wrong. Beauvoir's existentialist ethics, on the other hand, does explain why it is wrong. In her critique of Beauvoir's concept of transcendence, Lundgren-Gothlin remarks: "there should be a distinction between a true, authentic, fulfilled transcendence and an inauthentic transcendence."[12] In *The Ethics of Ambiguity* Beauvoir does describe an authentic mode of transcendence: it is what she calls moral freedom, which serves as an ethical ideal that all should seek. Unfortunately, this concept of an authentic transcendence is largely missing from *The Second Sex*.

Beauvoir does seem to make one stab at least at explaining the moral fault involved in men's oppression of women. At the beginning of her chapter on myths Beauvoir starts out by postulating, in a Hegelian vein, that each subject is driven to set up an Other. In Hegel's scenario there are three possible outcomes to the struggle this sets off: the death or enslavement of one of the combatants, or the eventual establishment of reciprocity between them. To freely recognize another and have the other freely recognize you is obviously the ideal outcome, morally speaking. But to maintain this relation to others requires a constant tension, Beauvoir says, the same tension that living an authentic existence as a lack of being involves. This is one of the places in the text I mentioned earlier where Beauvoir reverts to some of the most important themes of *The Ethics of Ambiguity.*

Beauvoir then departs from Hegel's scenario to portray yet another possible outcome to this conflict.[13] If the subject is not up to assuming the burdens of maintaining authentic reciprocal relations to others, he (and Beauvoir sees most men to have taken this route) has the option of resorting to the half measure of setting himself up in relation to woman as the Other:

> She opposes him with neither the hostile silence of nature nor the nor the hard demands of a reciprocal relationship; she has the unique privilege of being a consciousness that it seems nonetheless possible to possess in the flesh. Thanks to her there is a way to escape from the implacable dialectic of master and slave which has its source in the reciprocity of freedoms. (DS I 232–33; TSS 141)

It is because women are consigned to immanence by male culture that men are able to take this way out.

In these passages Beauvoir tries to join the standpoint of existentialist ethics together with a Hegelian dialectic in order both to explain what motivates men's oppression of women and to judge it to be wrong. This behavior on the part of men is wrong because it is inauthentic. They are fleeing the challenge of establishing a free reciprocal relation with another human being by engaging in a relation with a being who is not, like them, a transcendence, but rather a being who is consigned to immanence. The implication is that one can only achieve authenticity by struggling to maintain free reciprocal relations with others. This ideal of authenticity bears a strong similarity to Beauvoir's ideal of moral freedom in *The Ethics of Ambiguity.* It is interesting that in order to explain what moral fault men commit in oppressing women here Beauvoir falls back upon this existentialist standard of authenticity.

The upshot of my analysis is that Beauvoir would have done better to have relied more on the philosophical framework that she set up in *The Ethics of Ambiguity* to supplement her new emphasis on the opposition between immanence and transcendence in *The Second Sex.*

If she had, she could have more easily answered two important questions that otherwise remain difficult for her. First, in what sense does the woman denied transcendence and consigned to immanence remain free? Secondly, why is men's exercise of their transcendence in oppressing women morally wrong?

Why did Beauvoir depart from the philosophical framework of her existentialist ethics in *The Second Sex* in this way? By the time that *Force of Circumstance* was published in 1963 she had come to reject completely the viewpoint of her earlier writings on ethics, although not for good reasons, I hold. I do not think that this process was already underway by 1949 when she finished *The Second Sex*. A careful reading of *The Second Sex* reveals important connections between it and *The Ethics of Ambiguity*. But there remains a tension between the conceptual schema of transcendence and immanence she relies on there and her postulation of different levels of freedom in *The Ethics of Ambiguity*. This tension is not a reason to reject either work. Everyone recognizes the importance of *The Second Sex*. *The Ethics of Ambiguity* is not so well known. But the conception Beauvoir develops there of a specifically moral level of freedom has an important contribution to make to theorizing oppression in general and women's oppression in particular.

Conclusion

I hope that the foregoing analysis demonstrates the extent to which philosophical themes permeate Beauvoir's writings. Why in spite of this did Beauvoir always insist she was not a philosopher? There are various ways to approach this puzzle. One could question Beauvoir's motives for making this assertion. Or one could approach it from a more philosophical angle and ask what, after all, *is* a philosopher?

Beauvoir thought that a philosopher was someone who created a philosophical system, as Sartre did in *Being and Nothingness.* That was one reason she saw Sartre to be a philosopher and not herself. Rather than creating a philosophical system, Beauvoir developed a philosophical point of view from which to approach a range of diverse phenomena, some usually considered beyond the purview of philosophy, for instance, the details of everyday experience she analyzed in her novels. This philosophical perspective evolved over time. One can locate various tensions, even inconsistencies, in it, that she never directly faced, perhaps because she never fit her philosophical ideas together into a system.

Instead of being put off by this loose-ended quality of Beauvoir's philosophical thought, I have found myself drawn in by it. With a philosophical system like the one Sartre laid out in *Being and Nothingness*, someone can elucidate it and then either defend or attack it. A number of philosophers choose to attack Sartre's existentialism. But it has fierce defenders too, many of whom point out how little its most virulent critics understand it. Still, it is interesting how much has been written about Sartrean *ethics,* specifically. It is interesting because, as I discussed in chapter 5, Sartre actually published extremely little on ethics. (The unpublished material only began to appear as these books on Sartrean ethics were being written.) Perhaps it was the open-ended and unfinished nature of Sartre's thought on this topic that drew these authors in as well.

The philosophy Beauvoir presents us with in her work is not a system. It is more like a system under construction. I think that this is the lure for someone writing on her philosophy. One feels invited to join in the project—to contribute an idea or two, even tentatively suggest a structural revision. This vision of philosophy as a joint project undertaken by author and commentator fits in with what Beauvoir says is true of all significant endeavors: the human world of meanings and values is created in tandem with others. This vision of philosophy as a joint undertaking also offers a model for understanding the intellectual relationship between Beauvoir and Sartre themselves. Of course, the social conditions that Beauvoir writes about in *The Second Sex* cannot help but have had an impact on what the division of labor is perceived to be when such a project is jointly undertaken by a man and a woman.

Another reason that writers on Sartre may have been drawn to write about something Sartre did not say much about—ethics—is that existentialism offers an intriguing perspective from which to approach ethics. It is true that existentialism's claim that all values, even ethical values, are creations of human freedom at first seems to undercut ethics. Yet, significantly, the challenge existentialism presents to morality turns out to be similar to the challenge our present historical situation presents to it. Can we look to any one authority or authoritative principle in our secular, culturally diverse, rapidly evolving society to provide an unshakeable foundation for moral values? I think not. If so, then we are on own, left to our own devices, just as existentialism tells us we are. Existentialist ethics, which attempts to show us that we do generate moral guidelines on our own, seems a promising direction in which to turn for help.

Existentialist ethics is appealing for another reason. It seems to mesh with actual moral experience. Ethical considerations enter into many decisions of major and minor import that we make throughout our lives. When faced with such decisions, even people with philosophical training do not drop everything and rush to the bookshelf.

There are great intellectual rewards in studying the ethical systems of Kant and utilitarianism, among others. But are the moral guidelines that they lay out the guidelines that most people follow in making ethical decisions? John Stuart Mill and Immanuel Kant would say so. But I wonder.

Both Beauvoir and Sartre point out that principles like the categorical imperative can be used to justify different courses of action (although not every possible course of action). If one applies any principle, one must choose first how to apply it. But many people do not even get to this step. In making ethical decisions they fly by the seat of the pants, as it were. In place of rational principles, emotions, others' reactions, memories, even hunches play a role in making up their minds. They do what *feels* right to them. I think that existentialist ethics is a promising philosophical approach to ethics because it seems to come the closest to capturing this feature of moral experience. Of course, a person who acts according to what feels right to her could turn out to do something that is very wrong. But one can fail to apply the categorical imperative in the correct way too. No philosophical system of ethics rules out the possibility of moral error. What is more significant to my mind is that a person can do something because it feels right to her *and* do the right thing. (I am refraining here from considering how anyone could actually know whether it is the right thing to do.) How? By accident? By luck? Out of habit? Through mystical intuition? Existentialist ethics says that it is essentially by making a leap in the dark. That does not mean that there are no reasons for what people do in these cases. There are plenty of reasons. The question is how someone determines what reasons to give weight to.

Existentialist ethics stresses honesty above all else. For it the most important factors in making moral decisions are who you are, which includes your relations to others and to the world, and the exact nature of the situation you face. These are factors you must honestly appraise. The opportunities for self-deception are endless, as are the temptations to engage in it. It is particularly hard (Sartre might say impossible) to be honest with yourself about yourself. But that does not mean that you should not try. Existentialist ethics is demanding in this regard. But it does justice to some people's moral experience in this way as well. It was Socrates who said that the unexamined life is not worth living.

Beauvoir's existentialist ethics is particularly appealing because it adds a concern with others to this ideal of personal honesty. Kant says that we have duties to ourselves, as well as to others. And some demands of morality do seem to concern only ourselves—the injunction to be honest with ourselves, for instance. However, the general consensus is that how we treat others is even more important, morally speaking. We feel that it is wrong to do certain things to other people, as well as wrong not to do certain things for them. But what determines what these things are?

Beauvoir's ethics tells us that we should be concerned about other people's freedom. This answer sounds promising. When deciding how to treat others it seems important to take into account how they want to be treated. It is not just that we should let them alone. We feel that we should help them, if we can, to do what they want to do, to engage in the activities and relationships that they value, so long as it does not infringe on others in turn.

But to say that we should be concerned with others' freedom seems rather empty. What does it mean to be free? The work that this book centers on, *The Ethics of Ambiguity,* has an important contribution to make to existentialism and to philosophy generally because it attempts to answer this question. I have named three different conceptions of freedom that I find in Beauvoir's text. First, there is ontological freedom, which Sartre claims, and Beauvoir accepts, all human beings always possess. This type of freedom is similar to what philosophers call freedom of the will. Since this freedom cannot be taken away from one, it is not something we have to worry about depriving others of. It is a morally significant feature of human beings, nonetheless, because it distinguishes them from other categories of being that we treat differently.

The second sort of freedom, which Beauvoir calls power, is a more concrete sort of freedom—the freedom to do and have things. It initially does seem important to questions of how we should treat others. To those steeped in the liberal democratic tradition it seems evident that we should constrain others' concrete freedom as little as possible. But it turns out to matter greatly what these other people do with their concrete freedom. Power can be used for ill or for good. So the goal we should aim for in our treatment of others cannot be merely to increase their concrete freedom.

Here is where the type of freedom I call moral freedom enters into the picture. Moral freedom, like concrete freedom, is the freedom to

engage oneself in the world. But, unlike concrete freedom, it is a freedom that engages in the world with others in certain particular ways.
What particular ways? It is somewhat difficult to pin down. Let me use
a rather simplistic example.

When I turn on my television, I have the freedom to choose
among more than sixty channels to watch. This is the freedom to do
something that has no long-term significance to me. My being able to
make this choice has no impact on anyone's future. If I were deprived
of this choice, I might not be pleased, but my life would not be
robbed of value or meaning. This is an example of a certain power I
have, a power bestowed on me by the technological advances made by
my culture.

I also had the freedom to apply to and try to graduate from graduate school in philosophy. At one point in history, more recently than
you might think, women did not have this freedom. My freedom to
attend graduate school did prove to be of long-term significance to
me. It had a decisive impact on my future. Educational opportunities
like this present someone with the opportunity to develop moral freedom in Beauvoir's conception of it. They do not insure that someone
will develop moral freedom. Moral freedom creates more opportunities for action for oneself and others, instead of closing them off or
remaining neutral to them. In deciding how to treat others we should
be concerned with how they can come to have this sort of freedom,
according to Beauvoir.

We should also be concerned with whether we ourselves can
achieve this type of freedom, both for moral and self-interested reasons. Happily, it turns out that our desire to realize moral freedom
ourselves and our desire that others be able to realize it can be satisfied by the same means. As Beauvoir says: "To will oneself free is also
to will others free" (EA 73). I need others to be free so that I can be
free myself.

This conception of a specifically moral level of freedom is not a
new one in the history of philosophy. Kant and Rousseau both develop a conception of moral freedom.[1] Beauvoir was undoubtedly influenced by Kant in her treatment of freedom in *The Ethics of
Ambiguity*.[2] But her conception of moral freedom is worlds away
from both Rousseau and Kant. Besides, her innovation was to introduce this idea of freedom into existentialism.

Beauvoir's innovative conception of moral freedom has been
overlooked by writers both on her work and on existentialist ethics,

which is why I have stressed it here. I think that it alone has the potential to put existentialist ethics on a sound philosophical footing. For it alone clears up a number of philosophical puzzles that arise from the original existentialist conception of freedom. In my judgment that represents quite an accomplishment for a woman who was "not a philosopher."

Notes

Chapter 1: Why Beauvoir's Ethics?

1. See, for instance, Risieri Frondizi, "Sartre's Early Ethics: A Critique" in *The Philosophy of Jean-Paul Sartre*, ed. Paul Arthur Schilpp (La Salle: Open Court, 1981) and Mary Warnock, *Existentialist Ethics* (New York: St. Martin's Press, 1967).

2. Karen Vintges, *Philosophy as Passion: The Thinking of Simone de Beauvoir*, trans. Anne Lavelle (Bloomington, IN: Indiana University Press, 1996), 89.

3. Vintges, 74, 82.

4. See my discussion of this method offered by Beauvoir in chapter 6.

5. Debra Bergoffen, *The Philosophy of Simone de Beauvoir* (Albany: State University of New York Press, 1997), 12.

6. Bergoffen, 76.

7. Bergoffen, 93, 97.

8. Eva Lundgren-Gothlin, *Sex and Existence*, trans. Linda Schenk (Hanover, NH: Wesleyan University Press, 1996), 252, 232.

9. Karen Vintges, on the other hand, does recognize that Beauvoir makes a distinction between ontological freedom and moral freedom in *The Ethics of Ambiguity*. See Vintges, 56.

10. See Lundgren-Gothlin, 240.

11. Sonia Kruks, *Situation and Human Existence* (London: Unwin Hyman, 1990), 90.

12. See Sonia Kruks, "Comments on Kristana Arp: 'Conceptions of Freedom in Beauvoir's *The Ethics of Ambiguity*,'" *International Studies in Philosophy* 31, no. 2 (1999).

13. Kruks, *Situation and Human Existence*, 98.

14. See Jean-Paul Sartre, *Being and Nothingness*, trans. Hazel E. Barnes (New York: Philosophical Library, 1956), 550. Sartre later gave up this idea. See Simone de Beauvoir, *Adieux: A Farewell to Sartre*, trans. Patrick O'Brian (New York: Pantheon Books, 1984), 352.

15. Sartre also discussed the freedom of others in *Being and Nothingness* and suggested that there is a connection between one's own freedom and the freedom of others in *Anti-Semite and Jew*, published in 1946. But he did not focus on this topic until later, starting in *Notebooks for an Ethics* and culminating in *The Critique of Dialectical Reason*.

Chapter 2: Beauvoir as Situated Subject: The Historical Background

1. Martin Heidegger, *Being and Time*, trans. John Macquarrie and Edward Robinson (New York: Harper & Row, Publishers, 1962), 60. His emphasis.

2. See Jean-Paul Sartre, *The Transcendence of the Ego*, trans. Forest Williams and Robert Kirkpatrick (New York: The Noonday Press, 1957).

3. The phenomenological origins of this work are covered over by the English translation. Parshley translates this phrase, for instance, as "Woman's Life Today."

4. See Margaret A. Simons, "Does Beauvoir's Philosophy Begin with Sartre?" in Margaret A. Simons, *Beauvoir and The Second Sex: Feminism, Race, and the Origins of Existentialism* (Lanham, MD: Rowman & Littlefield Publishers, Inc., 1999).

5. See Simone de Beauvoir "Littérature et métaphysique," in *L'Existentialisme et la sagesse des nations* (Paris: Les Éditions Nagel, 1986), 101.

6. See Jeffner Allen, "Simone de Beauvoir" in *Encyclopedia of Phenomenology*, ed. Lester Embree, et al. (Dordrecht: Kluwer Academic Publishers, 1997), 51.

7. Simone de Beauvoir, *The Prime of Life*, trans. Peter Green (Cleveland: The World Publishing Company, 1962), 122, 162. Summarizing Sartre's argument in *The Transcendence of the Ego* she says, "he outlined—in a Husserlian perspective but contrary to some of Husserl's most recent theories—the relationship between the self and the conscious mind . . ." *The Prime of Life*, 147. Of course, she would have to know what Husserl's theories were to say this.

8. Beauvoir told Margaret Simons this in an interview when talking about the composition of *The Second Sex*, which she started right after she finished *The Ethics of Ambiguity*. Margaret A. Simons, *Beauvoir and The Second Sex: Feminism, Race, and the Origins of Existentialism*, 94.

9. Simone de Beauvoir, *Adieux: A Farewell to Sartre*, trans. Patrick O'Brian (New York: Pantheon Books, 1984), 172.

10. Simone de Beauvoir, "La Phénoménologie de la perception de Maurice Merleau-Ponty," *Les Temps modernes* 1 (1945): 363.

11. For instance, Toril Moi argues that troubles in her relationship with Sartre affected the composition of *The Ethics of Ambiguity.* "It is when unspoken suffering blocks Beauvoir's creativity that her language grows flat and her accents lifeless and her syntax loses its bite." Toril Moi, *Simone de Beauvoir: The Making of an Intellectual Woman* (Cambridge: Blackwell Publishers, 1994), 250.

12. *The Prime of Life*, 121, 116.

13. *The Prime of Life*, 111.

14. Eva Lundgren-Gothlin, *Sex and Existence*, trans. Linda Schenck (Hanover, NH: Wesleyan University Press, 1996), 27, 264.

15. *The Prime of Life*, 267.

16. See *The Prime of Life*, 120.

17. "Perhaps Sartre suspected the truth, but could not bring himself to face the sinister reality he had been unable to escape during his nine months in Berlin—that Nazism was spreading right across Europe, and was far less of a mere "straw fire" than the Communists asserted." *The Prime of Life*, 156–57.

18. *The Prime of Life*, 220.

19. *The Prime of Life*, 285.

20. *The Prime of Life*, 295.

21. *The Prime of Life*, 285.

22. *The Prime of Life*, 424.

23. *The Prime of Life*, 384.

24. Susan Suleiman criticizes Beauvoir's obliviousness about the second action and her evasions over the first. What strikes Suleiman most strongly is that for her as a Jew "had I been in her place, I would not have had the choice of signing the oath or working for Radio-Paris." Susan Suleiman, "Simone de Beauvoir's Wartime Writings," *Contentions* (Winter 1992): 4.

25. *The Prime of Life*, 396.

26. *The Prime of Life*, 289.

27. *The Prime of Life*, 373.

28. See Deirdre Bair, *Simone de Beauvoir: A Biography* (New York: Summit Books, 1990), 293.

29. *The Prime of Life*, 473.

30. *The Prime of Life*, 473.

31. Lundgren-Gothlin, 38.

32. Lundgren-Gothlin, 39.

33. She writes in a letter to Sartre: "Kanapa [the editor of a Communist journal] has done an article in which he attacks you on the plane of philosophy of history. Actually its mainly me he's attacking, and in Tunis I want to write a long article about an ethics of finitude: about action and finitude, against their myth of the future and progress." Simone de Beauvoir, *Letters to Sartre*, trans. Quintin Hoare (New York: Little, Brown and Company, 1992), 402.

34. In *Force of Circumstance* she remarks, "My seventy-second birthday is now as close as the Liberation Day that happened yesterday." Simone de

Beauvoir, *Force of Circumstance*, trans. Richard Howard (New York: G. P. Putnam's Sons, 1964), 656.

35. See *Force of Circumstance*, 649.

36. *Force of Circumstance*, 654.

37. *Force of Circumstance*, 67.

Chapter 3: The Works Before *The Ethics of Ambiguity*

1. Simone de Beauvoir, *The Prime of Life*, trans. Peter Green (Cleveland: The World Publishing Company, 1962), 433.

2. Simone de Beauvoir, *She Came to Stay* (New York: W. W. Norton & Company, 1990). Translation modified.

3. *She Came to Stay*, 291.

4. "As with all of de Beauvoir's early fiction, the reader of *She Came to Stay* feels that the inspiration of the book was simply de Beauvoir's decision to show how Sartre's abstract principles could be made to work out in 'real life'." Hazel Barnes, "Self Encounter in *She Came to Stay*" in *Simone de Beauvoir: A Critical Reader*, ed. Elizabeth Fallaize, (London: Routledge, 1998), 158. Another pair of writers see this similarity as a proof that Sartre's theory of self-other relations comes from this novel, not vice versa. See Kate and Edward Fullbrook, *Simone de Beauvoir and Jean-Paul Sartre: The Remaking of a Twentieth-Century Legend* (New York: Basic Books, 1994).

5. *The Prime of Life*, 428.

6. See Deirdre Bair, *Simone de Beauvoir: A Biography* (New York: Summit Books, 1990), 639, note 28. This ordering of events explains why the essay is dedicated to "that lady" ("à cette dame"), which was Beauvoir's pet name for her and Sartre's friend Madame Morel, with whom they were staying in the south of France in September 1942.

7. See "Of the inequality that is between us" in *The Complete Works of Montaigne*, ed. and trans. Donald M. Frame (Stanford: Stanford University Press, 1957), 189.

8. "Since man is project, his happiness like his pleasures can only be projects" (PC 28).

9. Such 'name-dropping' is a common feature of the essay form she is writing in. Heidegger's ideas are given much more attention than are Sartre's. Beauvoir even ascribes the insight that for humans one's existence defines one's essence to Heidegger here. See PC 82.

10. Alice Schwarzer, *After The Second Sex: Conversations with Simone de Beauvoir*, trans. Marianne Howarth (New York: Pantheon Books, 1984), 109.

11. William McBride, *Sartre's Political Theory* (Bloomington, IN: Indiana University Press, 1991), 5.

12. Simone de Beauvoir, *Force of Circumstance*, trans. Richard Howard (New York: G. P. Putnam's Sons, 1964), 51. Apparently the premiere of *Les Bouches inutiles* took place on the same day as Sartre's lecture "Existentialism is a Humanism" did. Deirdre Bair found an October 29 date for the premiere of *Les Bouches inutiles* inscribed on a scrapbook at a library in Paris. See Bair, 643. Annie Cohen-Solal quotes from the original invitation for the "Existentialism is a Humanism" lecture, which has the date as Monday, October 29, 1945. See Annie Cohen-Solal, *Sartre: A Life*, trans. Norman Macafee (New York: Pantheon Books, 1987), 27. Contat and Rybalka, however, list the date of the lecture as Monday, October 28, 1945. But October 28 fell on a Sunday that year. See Michel Contat and Michel Rybalka, *The Writings of Jean-Paul Sartre*, Vol. 1 (Evanston: Northwestern University Press, 1974), 132.

13. *Force of Circumstance*, 51.

14. Simone de Beauvoir, *The Prime of Life*, 464. Beauvoir also used an incident like this in her novel *All Men Are Mortal*. See AMM 76ff.

15. See Bair, 273, 277.

16. See BO 224–25.

17. See Susan Suleiman, "Simone de Beauvoir's Wartime Writings," *Contentions* (Winter 1992): 15.

18. *She Came to Stay*, 12.

19. "I sat with him through his last moments, and watched the grim, protracted struggle with which life extinguishes finally itself, vainly trying to grasp the mystery of this departure to no destination. I stayed a long while alone with him when he had breathed his last; at first, though dead, he was still *there*, it was my father, but then he receded dizzily from me as I watched, and I found myself bent over a mere corpse." *The Prime of Life*, 389.

20. In her memoirs Beauvoir writes about how she intended Hélène's speech "to release him from his scruples." *The Prime of Life*, 429.

21. *Force of Circumstance*, 68.

22. Camus claimed that he signed it only because of his opposition to the death penalty. See Alice Kaplan, *The Collaborator* (Chicago: The University of Chicago Press, 2000), 198.

23. Detracting from its value as journalism is the fact that it appeared in print more than one year after Brasillach was executed on February 6, 1945.

24. "*Je Suis Partout* published a column each week entitled "Partout et ailleurs" [Everywhere and elsewhere], revealing the identities and locations of those who were trying to save themselves." Kaplan, 32.

25. The initial impetus for writing it was a request from Camus to contribute an "essay on action" to a series on existentialism. See Simone de Beauvoir, *Letters to Sartre*, trans. Quintin Hoare (New York: Little, Brown and Company, 1991), 393 and *Force of Circumstance*, 67.

26. See *Force of Circumstance*, 67.

27. She describes its nice pale blue cover in a letter to Nelson Algren dated November 8, 1947. See Simone de Beauvoir, *A Transatlantic Love Affair*, ed. Sylvie Le Bon de Beauvoir (New York: The New Press, 1998), 96.

Chapter 4: Willing Others Free: *The Ethics of Ambiguity*

1. Robert Parker, "Myths of Early Athens" in *Interpretations of Greek Mythology*, ed. Jan Bremmer (Totowa, NJ: Barnes & Noble Books, 1986), 193. See also Benjamin Powell, *Athenian Mythology: Erichthonius & the Three Daughters of Cecrops* (Chicago: Ares Publishers Inc., 1976) for more discussion of the myth.

2. See IMRP 49.

3. Francis Jeanson, *Sartre and the Problem of Morality*, trans. Robert V. Stone (Bloomington, IN: Indiana University Press, 1980), 15.

4. I do not read Beauvoir as holding, à la Sartre in *Being and Nothingness*, that a human is always an object for another consciousness.

5. I am not asserting that the existence of "eternal" truths depends on the existence of the body, or even on the existence of human beings. I am only claiming that our awareness of these truths is dependent on the functioning of the human body.

6. Thus Beauvoir is making a point similar to the one Kant develops at much greater length in his Second Critique, where he argues from the "fact" of morality to the existence of human freedom.

7. Francis Jeanson also considers the recognition of the fundamental ambiguity of human existence to be the main accomplishment of existentialism, but surprisingly enough, he does not refer to Beauvoir at all in this context, even though he titles the third part of his book (written after *The Ethics of Ambiguity* was finished) "Toward the Morality of Ambiguity." Jeanson, 175. See also 15.

8. Notice, however, that here Sartre does not stress that humans must make themselves a lack of being; they already are it.

9. "Consciousness can always pass beyond the existent, not toward its being, but toward the meaning of this being" (BN lxiii).

10. Simone de Beauvoir, "La Phénoménologie de la perception de Maurice Merleau-Ponty," *Les Temps modernes* 1 (October 1945): 366–67.

11. "Certain of the nothingness of this other, it explicitly affirms that this nothingness is *for it* the truth of the other; it destroys the independent object." G. W. F. Hegel, *Phenomenology of Spirit*, trans. A. V. Miller (Oxford: Clarendon Press, 1977), 109.

12. See BO 186 and Albert Camus, *Lyrical and Critical Essays*, trans. Ellen Conroy Kennedy (New York: Alfred Knopf, 1969), 160.

13. I am indicating the pages of the French original first and then the pages of the English translation. The translations, for the most part, are my own.

14. It must be noted, though, that in the next passage, using the example of the skier on the slope that Sartre also uses, Beauvoir reverts to a metaphor of domination: "I cannot appropriate the snow field where I slide. It remains foreign, forbidden, but I take delight in this very effort toward an impossible possession" (EA 12).

15. The phrase in the original French is "liberté morale." The translator translates this as ethical freedom, but I prefer to use the term moral freedom.

16. Commentators on Sartre use this term in the same sense. See Thomas R. Flynn, *Sartre and Marxist Existentialism* (Chicago: The University of Chicago Press, 1984) and David Detmer, *Freedom as a Value* (La Salle: Open Court, 1986).

17. See, for instance, Toril Moi, *Simone de Beauvoir: The Making of an Intellectual Woman* (Cambridge: Blackwell Publishers, 1994).

18. Hannah Arendt, *Eichmann in Jerusalem* (New York: Penguin Books, 1977), 50.

19. Arendt, 30.

20. Arendt, 49. For instance, Arendt recounts Eichmann's macabre testimony about a "normal human encounter" he had in a concentration camp with a man who had once been his contact in the Jewish community: "It was a great inner joy to me that I could at least see the man with whom I had worked so many years, and that we could speak with each other." 51.

21. Apparently Sartre was also an admirer of Lawrence. A headline in the newspaper *Combat* announced that when Sartre gave the lecture that was subsequently edited and published as "Existentialism is a Humanism" he proclaimed "Lawrence of Arabia an Existentialist." See Annie Cohen-Solal, *Sartre: A Life,* trans. Norman Macafee (New York: Pantheon Books, 1987), 252.

22. See the translators' note in Martin Heidegger, *Being and Time,* trans. John Macquarrie and Edward Robinson (New York: Harper & Row, Publishers, 1962), 105–6.

23. See Heidegger, 263. Interestingly, though, conscience actively discloses. See Heidegger, 314.

24. *The Prime of Life,* 434.

25. See "La Phénoménologie de la perception de Maurice Merleau-Ponty."

26. "if division and violence define war, the world has always been at war and always will be" (EA 119).

Chapter 5: Beauvoir's Ethics as an Existentialist Ethics

1. See Alice Schwarzer, *After The Second Sex,* trans. Marianne Howarth (New York: Pantheon Books, 1984), 109 and Margaret A. Simons, "Beauvoir Interview (1979)" in Margaaret A. Simons, *Beauvoir and The Second Sex: Feminism, Race and the Orgins of Existentialism* (Lanham, MD: Rowman & Littlefield Publishers, 1999).

2. Kate and Edward Fullbrook, *Simone de Beauvoir and Jean-Paul Sartre: The Remaking of a Twentieth-Century Legend* (New York: Basic Books, 1994).

3. See "Beauvoir's Early Philosophy: The 1927 Diary (1998)" in Simons, *Beauvoir and The Second Sex.*

4. See Hazel E. Barnes, *The Story I Tell Myself* (Chicago: The University of Chicago Press, 1997), 187–88 and Hazel Barnes, "Response to Margaret Simons," *Philosophy Today* 42 (Supplement 1998): 29–34.

5. See *Schwarzer*, 109.

6. See Simone de Beauvoir, *Force of Circumstance*, trans. Richard Howard (New York: G. P. Putnam's Sons, 1964), 199 and "Jean-Paul Sartre s'explique sur *Les Mots*," *Le Monde*, April 18, 1964 quoted in Hazel E. Barnes, *An Existentialist Ethics*, 2nd ed. (Chicago: The University of Chicago Press, 1978), 30–31.

7. See Robert V. Stone and Elizabeth A. Bowman, "Dialetical Ethics: A First Look at Sartre's Unpublished 1964 Rome Lecture Notes," *Social Text* 13/14 (Winter/Spring 1986): 195–215.

8. Philip Thody, for one, detects three different attitudes Sartre takes towards moral action in his novels and plays, but sees Sartre as switching back and forth between them in different works. See P. M. W. Thody, "Sartre and the Concept of Moral Action: The Example of his Novels and Plays," in *The Philosophy of Jean-Paul Sartre*, ed. Paul Arthur Schilpp (La Salle: Open Court, 1981), 422 ff.

9. Simone de Beauvoir, *Letters to Sartre*, trans. Quintin Hoare (New York: Little, Brown and Company, 1992), 391. The French word is "corriger," which can mean merely to copy-edit. See Simone de Beauvoir, *Lettres à Sartre, 1940–1963*, ed. Sylvie Le Bon de Beauvoir (Paris: Gallimard, 1990), 260. Of course by this time Sartre had come to rely heavily on Beauvoir's feedback on his writing. See Deirdre Bair, *Simone de Beauvoir: A Biography* (New York: Summit Books, 1990), 228.

10. See Annie Cohen-Solal, *Sartre: A Life*, trans. Norman Macafee (New York: Pantheon Books, 1987), 278.

11. See, Cohen-Solal 250–51. Contat and Rybalka report, on the other hand, that the printed version was a "slightly altered version" of the original lecture. Michel Contat and Michel Rybalka, *The Writings of Jean-Paul Sartre*, Vol. 1 (Evanston: Northwestern University Press, 1974), 132–33.

12. Alexandre Astruc and Michel Contat, *Sartre by Himself*, trans. Richard Seaver (New York: Urizen Books, 1978), 74–75.

13. I discovered that the most widely used English translation of this work leaves out sentences and mistranslates key words. I therefore quote from my own translation, but cite the pages the passages are on in the English translation in the notes. Jean-Paul Sartre, *L'Existentialisme est une humanisme* (Paris: Les Éditions Nagel, 1970), my translation, 28. Jean-Paul Sartre, *Existentialism and Human Emotions* (New York: Philosophical Library, 1957), 18.

14. *L'Existentialisme est une humanisme*, 26, *Existentialism and Human Emotions*, 17.

15. Peter Caws, *Sartre* (London: Routledge & Kegan Paul, 1979), 121.

16. *L'Existentialisme est une humanisme*, 27, *Existentialism and Human Emotions*, 18.

17. *L'Existentialisme est une humanisme*, 47, *Existentialism and Human Emotions*, 28.

18. *L'Existentialisme est une humanisme*, 49, *Existentialism and Human Emotions*, 29.

19. *L'Existentialisme est une humanisme*, 87, *Existentialism and Human Emotions*, 48.

20. *L'Existentialisme est une humanisme*, 88–89, *Existentialism and Human Emotions*, 48.

21. See, for instance, David Detmer, *Freedom as a Value* (La Salle: Open Court, 1986), 137.

22. *L'Existentialisme est une humanisme*, 43, *Existentialism and Human Emotions*, 26.

23. *L'Existentialisme est une humanisme*, 66, *Existentialism and Human Emotions*, 37.

24. *L'Existentialisme est une humanisme*, 66, *Existentialism and Human Emotions*, 37. See PC 96.

25. *L'Existentialisme est une humanisme*, 82, *Existentialism and Human Emotions*, 44.

26. *L'Existentialisme est une humanisme*, 83–84, *Existentialism and Human Emotions*, 45–46.

27. Jean-Paul Sartre, *Notebooks for an Ethics*, trans. David Pellauer (Chicago: The University of Chicago Press, 1992), vii.

28. "In the Ethics there was an idea that I intended to develop, but never did. What I wrote was the first part which was supposed to introduce a main idea, and at that point I came up against a difficulty." Jean-Paul Sartre, *Life/Situations: Essays Written and Spoken*, trans. Paul Auster and Lydia Davis (New York: Pantheon Books, 1977), 74.

29. *Notebooks for an Ethics*, ix.

30. *Notebooks for an Ethics*, 279.

31. *Notebooks for an Ethics*, 280.

32. *Notebooks for an Ethics*, 281.

33. See, for instance, Norman N. Greene, *Jean-Paul Sartre: The Existentialist Ethic* (Ann Arbor: The University of Michigan Press, 1960) and Joseph S. Catalano, "A Sketch of Sartrean Ethics," in *Good Faith and Other Essays* (Lanham, MD: Rowman & Littlefield Publishers, Inc.: 1996).

34. Linda Bell, *Sartre's Ethics of Authenticity* (Tuscaloosa: The University of Alabama Press, 1989), 19.

35. Detmer, 2.

36. Thomas Anderson, *The Foundation and Structure of Sartrean Ethics* (Lawrence: The Regents Press of Kansas, 1979), 4.

37. See Anderson, *The Foundation and Structure of Sartrean Ethics*, 4 and Detmer, 180. Bell does not do this. Thomas Flynn, however, calls *The Ethics of Ambiguity* the "official commentary" on Sartre's existentialist ethics. Thomas R. Flynn, *Sartre and Marxist Existentialism* (Chicago: The University of Chicago Press, 1984), 39. In a later paper Anderson does distinguish between Beauvoir's and Sartre's approach to ethics. Although he still sees them as propounding the same ethics, he says that it is "to de Beauvoir that we owe the clearest and best reasoned presentation in print" of it. "Beauvoir's Influence on Sartre's First Ethics and Vice Versa," paper presented to the Society for Phenomenology and Existential Philosophy, October 1995.

38. Thomas Anderson writes, "In any case it is clear that Sartre never thought there was any incompatibility between insisting that man was ontologically free and at the same time advocating that he choose to realize his freedom more fully and concretely." Anderson, *The Foundation and Structure of Sartrean Ethics*, 55. David Detmer makes a similar distinction between ontological freedom and practical freedom and suggests that the enhancement of practical freedom is the goal in Sartre's ethics. See Detmer, 183.

39. *L'Existentialisme est une humanisme*, 83, *Existentialism and Human Emotions*, 46.

40. *L'Existentialisme est une humanisme*, 82, *Existentialism and Human Emotions*, 45.

41. *L'Existentialisme est une humanisme*, 82, *Existentialism and Human Emotions*, 45.

42. Richard Bernstein makes this objection. See Richard J. Bernstein, *Praxis and Action* (Philadelphia: University of Pennsylvania Press, 1971), 154–55.

43. See Flynn, 38.

44. Anderson, *The Foundation and Structure of Sartrean Ethics*, 46.

45. Anderson, *The Foundation and Structure of Sartrean Ethics*, 46–47.

46. Bell, 56.

47. Bell, 57.

48. Bell, 55.

49. Linda Bell was my commentator on a paper I gave to the Society for Phenomenology and Existential Philosophy in October, 1998, in which I first discussed these arguments. From her comments I learned that I had at first misunderstood her argument in particular. She has not seen or commented on my new interpretation of it.

50. *The Prime of Life,* 434. See also EA 113 where she declares that "the supreme end at which man must aim is his freedom, which alone is capable of establishing the value of every end."

51. Anderson, *The Foundation and Structure of Sartrean Ethics*, 54.

52. Anderson, *The Foundation and Structure of Sartrean Ethics*, 52.

53. Hazel E. Barnes, *An Existentialist Ethics* (Chicago: The University of Chicago Press, 1978), 49.

54. See Barnes, *An Existentialist Ethics*, 7.

55. See Barnes, *An Existentialist Ethics*, 8–9.

56. Barnes, *An Existentialist Ethics*, 19.

57. Barnes, *An Existentialist Ethics*, 19.

58. "We cannot call their position ethical inasmuch as it is based upon self-deception, but it is the very opposite of an open choice of the nonethical." Barnes, *An Existentialist Ethics*, 19. Later in the book, Barnes seems to take a contrary position on this question: "To choose to live unauthentically in bad faith is to choose the nonethical and to abandon all pretense of wanting to justify one's life." 60.

59. Mary Warnock, *Existentialist Ethics* (New York: St. Martin's Press, 1967), 54.

60. Alvin Plantinga, "An Existentialist's Ethics" in *Ethics*, ed. Julius R. Weinberg and Keith E. Yandell, (New York: Holt, Rinehart and Winston, 1971), 22–23.

61. "Good faith wishes to flee the 'not-believing-what-one-believes' by finding refuge in being" (BN 70).

62. This is not apparent in the English translation of the text, where "bad faith" is translated as "dishonesty" and "good faith" and "authenticity" as "honesty." See note 14.

63. Detmer, 165.

64. Jonathan Harrison, "Ethical Substance" in *The Encyclopedia of Philosophy*, Vol. 3, ed. Paul Edwards (New York: Macmillan, 1967), 78.

65. *The Prime of Life*, 429.

66. Bernard Williams, *Morality: An Introduction to Ethics* (Cambridge: Cambridge University Press, 1972), 15.

67. Williams, 27.

68. Williams, 35–36.

69. Detmer, 148.

70. *L'Existentialisme est une humanisme*, 47, *Existentialism and Human Emotions*, 28.

71. Gilbert Harman and Judith Jarvis Thompson, *Moral Relativism and Moral Objectivity* (Cambridge: Blackwell, 1996), 154.

72. See Detmer, 163.

73. Harman and Thompson, 154. She goes on to point out that even moral objectivism is compatible with a certain degree of moral indeterminacy. In this regard, as in the others I mention, Beauvoir's subjectivism is on a par with ethical objectivism.

Chapter 6: Beauvoir's Ethics as an Ethics of Political Liberation

1. See his collected essays in Jean-Paul Sartre, *"What is Literature?" and Other Essays* (Cambridge, MA: Harvard University Press, 1988).

2. Compare the optimism of this passage to the pessimistic statement later on: "if division and violence define war, the world has always been at war and always will be" (EA 119).

3. See, for instance, Anne Whitmarsh, *Simone de Beauvoir and the Limits of Commitment* (Cambridge: Cambridge University Press, 1981) and Genevieve Lloyd, *The Man of Reason* (Minneapolis: University of Minnesota Press, 1984).

4. Beauvoir had had this example of the harem slave in mind for some time when she wrote *The Ethics of Ambiguity*. In her memoirs she records a conversation she had with Sartre in 1940 in which she asked, "what sort of transcendence could a woman shut up in a harem achieve?" Simone de Beauvoir, *The Prime of Life*, trans. Peter Green (Cleveland: The World Publishing Company, 1962), 346.

5. "The spirit of seriousness considers health, riches, education, comfort as indisputable goods inscribed in the sky" (PC 91).

6. Later she seems to recognize that children cannot be likened to the oppressed: "Childhood is . . . a natural situation whose limits are not created by other men and which is thereby not comparable to a situation of oppression" (EA 141).

7. She ascribes this insight to Descartes and also refers to Descartes when she makes the distinction between power and freedom in *Pyrrhus et Cinéas*. See PC 86. In *Being and Nothingness* Sartre makes a similar distinction between "freedom of choice" and "freedom of obtaining" and traces it back to Descartes and the Stoics. See BN 484.

8. See EA 30–31.

9. Robert Stone, in one of the first philosophical treatments of Beauvoir's ethics, points out how Beauvoir's theory of freedom provides a basis for socialism by highlighting the need for a "material freedom from want that allows human relationships to flourish." He also notes that the writers' resistance group that Beauvoir joined in April 1941 was called "Socialism and Freedom." Robert Stone, "Simone de Beauvoir and the Existential Basis of Socialism" *Social Text* 17 (Fall 1987): 127.

10. Simone de Beauvoir, *1984 Britannica Book of the Year*, quoted in Deirdre Bair, *Simone de Beauvoir: A Biography* (New York: Summit Books, 1990), 546.

11. See PC 86.

12. Simone de Beauvoir, *Force of Circumstance*, trans. Richard Howard (New York: G.P. Putnam's Sons, 1964), 68.

13. See Kristana Arp, "Beauvoir's Concept of Bodily Alienation" in *Feminist Interpretations of Simone de Beauvoir*, ed. Margaret A. Simons (University Park: The Pennsylvania State University Press, 1995).

14. See Simone de Beauvoir, "La Phénoménologie de la perception de Maurice Merleau-Ponty," *Les Temps modernes* 1 (October 1945): 363–67. In *The Second Sex* she says, "However, one will say, in the perspective I am adopting—that of Heidegger, Sartre and Merleau-Ponty—if the body is not a *thing*, it is a situation; it is our grasp upon the world and the sketch of our projects" (DS I 72).

15. Jean-Jacques Rousseau, *The Social Contract*, trans. Maurice Cranston (Middlesex, England: Penguin Books, 1984), 64 (Book I, chap. 7).

16. To liberate someone who has no active desire to be liberated would be an act of psychological violence similar to the one Beauvoir alludes to committed by Gregers in Ibsen's play where by telling the truth he wipes out a lifetime of illusion. It only would be right in such a case, Beauvoir says, if one first creates a situation where the truth would be bearable. See EA 143.

17. This is not always true of moral freedom, though, because of its inter-penetration with others' moral freedom: "It is only by prolonging itself through the freedom of others that it [freedom] manages to surpass death itself" (EA 32). Beauvoir also says in *Pyrrhus et Cinéas* that "to kill a man is not to destroy him; all we only ever attain is the facticity of the other" (PC 116).

18. See *Force of Circumstance*, 68.

19. "Thus it is possible, and often it even happens, that one finds himself obliged to oppress and kill men who are pursuing goals whose validity one acknowledges himself" (EA 99).

20. See EA 150–51.

Chapter 7: Connections between *The Ethics of Ambiguity* and *The Second Sex*

1. See, for example, Margaret A. Simons, *Beauvoir and The Second Sex: Feminism, Race, and the Origins of Existentialism* (Lanham, MD: Rowman & Littlefield Publishers, Inc., 1999) and Michèle Le Doeuff, *Hipparchia's Choice*, trans. Trista Selous (Cambridge, MA: Basil Blackwell, 1991).

2. See Deirdre Bair, "Introduction to the Vintage Edition" in Simone de Beauvoir, *The Second Sex*, trans. H. M. Parshley (New York: Vintage Books, 1989), ix. In an endnote Bair tells us that this information was conveyed to her in one of a number of interviews she had with Beauvoir from 1981 to 1986. See xvii.

3. See Margaret A. Simons, "The Silencing of Simone de Beauvoir: Guess What's Missing from *The Second Sex*" in Margaret A. Simon, *Beauvoir and The Second Sex: Feminism, Race, and the Origins of Existentialism*. Beauvoir was great-ly concerned about this when Simons told her. See "Beauvoir Interview (1982)" in the same.

4. I am indicating the pages of the French original first and then the pages of the English translation. The translations, for the most part, are my own.

5. See, for instance, Judith Okely, *Simone de Beauvoir* (London: Virago, 1986).

6. See Michèle Le Doeuff, "Simone de Beauvoir and Existentialism," *Feminist Studies* 6 (1980): 277–89 and Genevieve Lloyd, *The Man of Reason* (Minneapolis: University of Minnesota Press, 1984).

7. See Kristana Arp, "Beauvoir's Concept of Bodily Alienation" in *Feminist Interpretations of Simone de Beauvoir*, ed. Margaret A. Simons (University Park: Pennsylvania State University Press, 1995).

8. See EA 25.

9. Sonia Kruks, *Situation and Human Existence* (London: Unwin Hyman, 1990), 102.

10. Kruks, *Situation and Human Existence*, 98.

11. Eva Lundgren-Gothlin, *Sex and Existence*, trans. Linda Schenk (Hanover, NH: Wesleyan University Press, 1996), 239.

12. Lundgren-Gothlin, 241.

13. Lundgren-Gothlin also points out how Beauvoir departs from Hegel here. See Lundgren-Gothlin, 72.

Conclusion

1. Kant argues that "a free will and a will under moral laws are identical." Immanuel Kant, *Foundations of the Metaphysics of Morals*, trans. Lewis White Beck (Indianapolis, IN: The Bobbs-Merrill Company, Inc., 1959), 65. In *The Social Contract* Rousseau speaks about moral freedom as well, saying, in a way that prefigures Kant: "obedience to a law one prescribes to oneself is freedom." Jean-Jacques Rousseau, *The Social Contract*, trans. Maurice Cranston (Middlesex, England: Penguin Books, 1968), 65. Book I, chap. 8.

2. She records how at the time that she wrote *The Ethics of Ambiguity* she used Kant as "a focal point or a sounding board" for her own philosophical ideas, much to Sartre's dismay. See Deirdre Bair, *Simone de Beauvoir: A Biography* (New York: Summit Books, 1990), 271.

Bibliography

Allen, Jeffner. "Simone de Beauvoir." In *Encyclopedia of Phenomenology*, edited by Lester Embree, et al. Dordrecht, The Netherlands: Kluwer Academic Publishers, 1997.

Anderson, Thomas. "Beauvoir's Influence on Sartre's First Ethics and Vice Versa." Paper delivered at The Society for Phenomenology and Existential Philosophy, Chicago, October 1995.

———. *The Foundation and Structure of Sartrean Ethics*. Lawrence, KS: The Regents Press of Kansas, 1979.

———. *Sartre's Two Ethics: From Authenticity to Integral Humanity*. Chicago: Open Court, 1993.

Arendt, Hannah. *Eichmann in Jerusalem*. New York: Penguin Books, 1977.

Arp, Kristana. "Beauvoir's Concept of Bodily Alienation." In *Feminist Interpretations of Simone de Beauvoir*, edited by Margaret A. Simons. University Park, PA: Pennsylvania State University Press, 1995.

———. "Beauvoir's Existentialist Ontology." *Philosophy Today* 43, no. 3 (Fall 1999): 266–71.

———. "Conceptions of Freedom in Beauvoir's *The Ethics of Ambiguity*." *International Studies in Philosophy* 31, no. 2 (1999): 25–34.

———. "A Different Voice in the Phenomenological Tradition: Simone de Beauvoir and the Ethic of Care." In *Feminist Phenomenology*, edited by Linda Fisher and Lester Embree. Dordrecht, The Netherlands: Kluwer Academic Publishers, 2000.

———. "Existentialism and the Ethics of Care." *American Philosophical Association Newsletter on Philosophy and Feminism* 95, no. 2 (Spring 1996): 41–43.

Astruc, Alexandre, and Michel Contat. *Sartre by Himself*. Translated by Richard Seaver. New York: Urizen Books, 1978.

Bair, Deirdre. *Simone de Beauvoir: A Biography*. New York: Summit Books, 1990.

Barnes, Hazel E. *An Existentialist Ethics*. 2nd ed. Chicago: The University of Chicago Press, 1978.

_____. "Response to Margaret Simons." *Philosophy Today* 42 (Supplement 1998): 29–34.

_____. "Self Encounter in *She Came to Stay*." In *Simone de Beauvoir: A Critical Reader*, edited by Elizabeth Fallaize. London: Routledge, 1998.

_____. *The Story I Tell Myself: A Venture in Existentialist Autobiography*. Chicago: The University of Chicago Press, 1997.

Beauvoir, Simone de. *Adieux: A Farewell to Sartre*. Translated by Patrick O'Brian. New York: Pantheon Books, 1984.

_____. *All Men Are Mortal*. Translated by Leonard N. Friedman. New York: W. W. Norton & Company, 1992.

_____. *The Blood of Others*. Translated by Roger Senhouse and Yvonne Moyse. New York: Pantheon Books, 1983.

_____. *The Ethics of Ambiguity*. Translated by Bernard Frechtman. New York: Carol Publishing Group, 1991. Translation of *Pour une morale de L'ambiguité*. Paris: Gallimard, 1947.

_____. *Force of Circumstance*. Translated by Richard Howard. New York: G. P. Putnam's Sons, 1964.

_____. "La Phénoménologie de la perception de Maurice Merleau-Ponty." *Les Temps modernes* 1 (1945): 363–67.

_____. *Letters to Sartre*. Edited and translated by Quintin Hoare. New York: Little, Brown and Company, 1992. Translation of *Lettres à Sartre*. 2 vols. Edited by Sylvie Le Bon de Beauvoir. Paris: Gallimard, 1990.

_____. *L'Existentialisme et la sagesse des nations*. Paris: Les Éditions Nagel, 1986.

_____. *The Prime of Life*. Translated by Peter Green. Cleveland: The World Publishing Company, 1962.

_____. *Pyrrhus et Cinéas*. Paris: Gallimard, 1944. 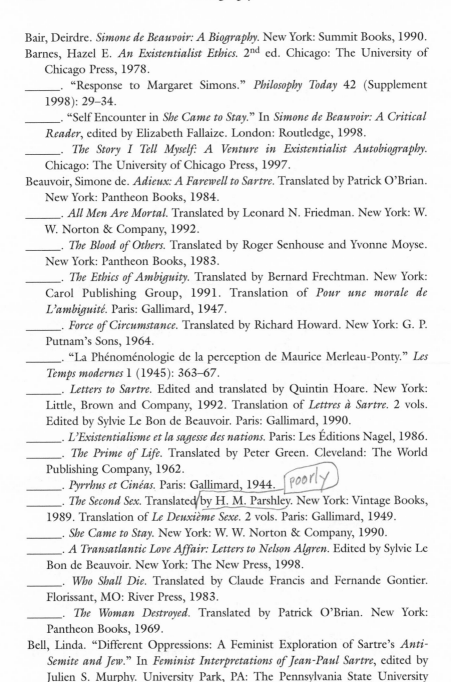 *poorly*

_____. *The Second Sex*. Translated by H. M. Parshley. New York: Vintage Books, 1989. Translation of *Le Deuxième Sexe*. 2 vols. Paris: Gallimard, 1949.

_____. *She Came to Stay*. New York: W. W. Norton & Company, 1990.

_____. *A Transatlantic Love Affair: Letters to Nelson Algren*. Edited by Sylvie Le Bon de Beauvoir. New York: The New Press, 1998.

_____. *Who Shall Die*. Translated by Claude Francis and Fernande Gontier. Florissant, MO: River Press, 1983.

_____. *The Woman Destroyed*. Translated by Patrick O'Brian. New York: Pantheon Books, 1969.

Bell, Linda. "Different Oppressions: A Feminist Exploration of Sartre's *Anti-Semite and Jew*." In *Feminist Interpretations of Jean-Paul Sartre*, edited by Julien S. Murphy. University Park, PA: The Pennsylvania State University Press, 1999.

_____. *Rethinking Violence in the Midst of Violence: A Feminist Approach to Freedom.* Lanham, MD: Rowman & Littlefield Publishers, Inc., 1993.

_____. *Sartre's Ethics of Authenticity.* Tuscaloosa, AL: The University of Alabama Press, 1989.

Bergoffen, Debra. "From Husserl to Beauvoir: Gendering the Perceiving Subject." In *Feminist Phenomenology,* edited by Linda Fisher and Lester Embree. Dordrecht, The Netherlands: Kluwer Academic Publishers, 2000.

_____. *The Philosophy of Simone de Beauvoir.* Albany, NY: State University of New York Press, 1997.

Bernstein, Richard J. *Praxis and Action.* Philadelphia: University of Pennsylvania Press, 1971.

Camus, Albert. *Lyrical and Critical Essays.* Translated by Ellen Conroy Kennedy. New York: Alfred Knopf, 1969.

Catalano, Joseph S. *Good Faith and Other Essays.* Lanham, MD: Rowman & Littlefield Publishers, Inc., 1996.

Caws, Peter. *Sartre.* London: Routledge & Kegan Paul, 1979.

Cohen-Solal, Annie. *Sartre: A Life.* Translated by Norman Macafee. New York: Pantheon Books, 1987.

Contat, Michel, and Michel Rybalka. *The Writings of Jean-Paul Sartre.* 2 Vols. Translated by Richard C. McCleary. Evanston: Northwestern University Press, 1974.

Detmer, David. *Freedom as a Value.* La Salle, IL: Open Court, 1986.

Edwards, Paul, ed. *The Encyclopedia of Philosophy.* New York: Macmillan, 1967.

Embree, Lester et al., eds. *Encyclopedia of Phenomenology.* Dordrecht, The Netherlands: Kluwer Academic Publishers, 1997.

Fallaize, Elizabeth. *The Novels of Simone de Beauvoir.* London: Routledge, 1990.

Elizabeth Fallaize, ed. *Simone de Beauvoir: A Critical Reader.* London: Routledge, 1998.

Flynn, Thomas R. *Sartre and Marxist Existentialism.* Chicago: The University of Chicago Press, 1984.

Francis, Claude and Fernande Gontier. *Les Écrits de Simone de Beauvoir.* Paris: Gallimard, 1979.

Frondizi, Risieri. "Sartre's Early Ethics: A Critique." In *The Philosophy of Jean-Paul Sartre,* edited by Paul Arthur Schilpp. La Salle, IL: Open Court, 1981.

Fullbrook, Kate and Edward. *Simone de Beauvoir and Jean-Paul Sartre: The Remaking of a Twentieth-Century Legend.* New York: Basic Books, 1994.

Greene, Norman N. *Jean-Paul Sartre: The Existentialist Ethic.* Ann Arbor: The University of Michigan Press, 1960.

Gordon, Lewis R. *Bad Faith and Anti-Black Racism.* Atlantic Highlands, NJ: Humanities Press, 1995.

Harman, Gilbert, and Judith Jarvis Thompson. *Moral Relativism and Moral Objectivity.* Cambridge: Blackwell, 1996.

Harris, Jonathan. "Ethical Subjectivism." In *The Encyclopedia of Philosophy*, edited by Paul Edwards. New York: Macmillan, 1967.

Hegel, G.W.F. *Phenomenology of Spirit*. Translated by A. V. Miller. Oxford: Clarendon Press, 1977.

Heidegger, Martin. *Being and Time*. Translated by John Macquarrie and Edward Robinson. New York: Harper & Row, Publishers, 1962.

Heinämaa, Sara. "Simone de Beauvoir's Phenomenology of Sexual Difference." *Hypatia* 14, no. 2 (Fall 1999): 114–32.

Holveck, Eleanore. "*The Blood of Others*: A Novel Approach to *The Ethics of Ambiguity*." *Hypatia* 14, no. 2 (Fall 1999): 3–17.

Jeanson, Francis. *Sartre and the Problem of Morality*. Translated by Robert V. Stone. Bloomington, IN: Indiana University Press, 1980.

Joseph, Gilbert. *Une si douce Occupation: Simone de Beauvoir et Jean-Paul Sartre 1940–1944*. Paris: Albin Michel, 1991.

Kant, Immanuel. *Foundations of the Metaphysics of Morals*. Translated by Lewis White Beck. Indianapolis, IN: The Bobbs-Merrill Company, Inc., 1959.

Kaplan, Alice. *The Collaborator: The Trial and Execution of Robert Brasillach*. Chicago: The University of Chicago Press, 2000.

Kruks, Sonia. "Beauvoir: The Weight of Situation." In *Simone de Beauvoir: A Critical Reader*, edited by Elizabeth Fallaize. London: Routledge, 1998.

_____. "Comments on Kristana Arp: 'Conceptions of Freedom in Beauvoir's *The Ethics of Ambiguity*'." *International Studies in Philosophy* 31, no. 2 (1999): 35–38.

_____. *Situation and Human Existence*. London: Unwin Hyman, 1990.

Le Doeuff, Michèle. *Hipparchia's Choice: An Essay Concerning Women, Philosophy, etc*. Translated by Trista Selous. Cambridge, MA: Basil Blackwell, 1991.

_____. "Simone de Beauvoir and Existentialism." *Feminist Studies* 6 (1980): 277–89.

Linsenbard, Gail E. "Beauvoir, Ontology and Women's Human Rights." *Hypatia* 14, no. 2 (Fall 1999): 145–62.

Lloyd, Genevieve. *The Man of Reason*. Minneapolis: University of Minnesota Press, 1984.

Lundgren-Gothlin, Eva. *Sex and Existence*. Translated by Linda Schenk. Hanover, NH: Wesleyan University Press, 1996.

McBride, William. *Sartre's Political Theory*. Bloomington, IN: Indiana University Press, 1991.

Moi, Toril. *Simone de Beauvoir: The Making of an Intellectual Woman*. Cambridge: Blackwell Publishers, 1994.

Montaigne, Michel de. *The Complete Works of Montaigne*. Edited and translated by Donald M. Frame. Stanford: Stanford University Press, 1957.

Okely, Judith. *Simone de Beauvoir*. London: Virago, 1986.

Olafson, Frederick A. *Principles and Persons: An Ethical Interpretation of Existentialism.* Baltimore, MD: The Johns Hopkins Press, 1967.

Parker, Robert. "Myths of Early Athens." In *Interpretations of Greek Mythology*, edited by Jan Bremmer. Totowa, NJ: Barnes & Noble Books, 1986.

Pelczynski, Zbigniew and John Gray, eds. *Conceptions of Liberty in Political Philosophy.* New York: St. Martin's Press, 1984.

Plantinga, Alvin. "An Existentialist's Ethics." In *Ethics*, edited by Julius R. Weinberg and Keith E. Yandell. New York: Holt, Rinehart and Winston, 1971.

Powell, Benjamin. *Athenian Mythology: Erichthonius & the Three Daughters of Cecrops.* Chicago: Ares Publishers Inc., 1976.

Rousseau, Jean-Jacques. *The Social Contract.* Translated by Maurice Cranston. Middlesex, England: Penguin Books, 1968.

Sartre, Jean-Paul. *Anti-Semite and Jew.* Translated by George J. Becker. New York: Grove Press, Inc., 1948.

_____. *Being and Nothingness.* Translated by Hazel E. Barnes. New York: Philosophical Library, 1956.

_____. "Existentialism." Translated by Bernard Frechtman. In *Existentialism and Human Emotions.* New York: Philosophical Library, 1957. Translation of *L'Existentialisme est une humanisme.* Paris: Les Éditions Nagel, 1970.

_____. *Life/Situations: Essays Written and Spoken.* Translated by Paul Auster and Lydia Davis. New York: Pantheon Books, 1977.

_____. *Notebooks for an Ethics.* Translated by David Pellauer. Chicago: The University of Chicago Press, 1992.

_____. *The Transcendence of the Ego.* Translated by Forest Williams and Robert Kirkpatrick. New York: The Noonday Press, 1957.

_____. *"What is Literature?" and Other Essays.* Cambridge, MA: Harvard University Press, 1988.

Schwarzer, Alice. *After The Second Sex: Conversations with Simone de Beauvoir.* Translated by Marianne Howarth. New York: Pantheon Books, 1984.

Simons, Margaret A. "An Appeal to Reopen the Question of Influence." *Philosophy Today* 42 (Supplement 1998): 17–24.

_____. *Beauvoir and The Second Sex: Feminism, Race, and the Origins of Existentialism.* Lanham. MD: Rowman & Littlefield Publishers, Inc., 1999.

Stone, Robert. "Simone de Beauvoir and the Existential Basis of Socialism." *Social Text* 17 (Fall 1987): 123–42.

Stone, Robert, and Elizabeth A. Bowman. "Dialectical Ethics: A First Look at Sartre's Unpublished 1964 Rome Lecture Notes." *Social Text* 13/14 (Winter/Spring 1986): 195–215.

Suleiman, Susan. *Risking Who One Is.* Cambridge, MA: Harvard University Press, 1994.

_____. "Simone de Beauvoir's Wartime Writings." *Contentions* (Winter 1992): 1–21.

Thody, P.M.W. "Sartre and the Concept of Moral Action: The Example of His Novels and Plays." In *The Philosophy of Jean-Paul Sartre*, edited by Paul Arthur Schilpp. La Salle, IL: Open Court, 1981.

Tidd, Ursula. "The Self-Other Relation in Beauvoir's Ethics and Autobiography." *Hypatia* 14, no. 2 (Fall 1999): 163–74.

Vintges, Karen. *Philosophy as Passion: The Thinking of Simone de Beauvoir*. Translated by Anne Lavelle. Bloomington, IN: Indiana University Press, 1996.

Warnock, Mary. *Existentialist Ethics*. New York: St. Martin's Press, 1967.

Whitmarsh, Anne. *Simone de Beauvoir and the Limits of Commitment*. Cambridge: Cambridge University Press, 1981.

Williams, Bernard. *Morality: An Introduction to Ethics*. Cambridge: Cambridge University Press, 1972.

Index